GOD'S INCREDIBLE MERCY

231.6
M29g

435

NOTRE DAME MOTHERHOUSE
320 EAST RIPA AVE.
READING ROOM
ST. LOUIS, MO 63125

GOD'S INCREDIBLE MERCY

George A. Maloney, SJ

ALBA · HOUSE   NEW · YORK
SOCIETY OF ST. PAUL, 2187 VICTORY BLVD., STATEN ISLAND, NEW YORK 10314

Library of Congress Cataloging-in-Publication Data

Maloney, George A., 1924 -
   God's incredible mercy / by George A. Maloney.
      p.   cm.
   ISBN 0-8189-0544-1
   1. God — Mercy.   I. Title.
BT153.M4M35   1989   88-30108
231'.6 — dc19   CIP

Imprimi Potest:
Patrick J. Burns, S.J.
Provincial, Wisconsin Province

Designed, printed and bound in the United States of America by the Fathers and Brothers of the Society of St. Paul, 2187 Victory Boulevard, Staten Island, New York 10314, as part of their communications apostolate.

© *Copyright 1989 by George A. Maloney, S.J.*

Printing Information:

Current Printing - first digit 1 2 3 4 5 6 7 8 9 10 11 12 13 14 15 16 17 18 19 20

Year of Current Printing - first year shown
     1989 1990 1991 1992 1993 1994 1995 1996 1997 1998 1999 2000 2001 2002 2003

DEDICATION

to
MARY ANN *and* RAY DURAY
and
BONNIE BURCHETT
living witness of God's Mercy
to others.

Acknowledgments

Sincere thanks to Mary Louis Leonard for typing this manuscript and proofreading it along with the assistance of Sister Joseph Agnes, S.C.H.

Thanks are due to the Bruce Publishing Company for permission to use its translation of the New Terstament as the basic text for N.T. citations: *The New Testament*, Part one: *The Four Gospels* translated by James A. Kleist, S.J. and Part Two: *Acts of the Apostles, Epistles and Apocalypse* translated by Joseph L. Lilly, C.M. (Milwaukee, WI: The Bruce Publishing Company, 1956). Also to Darton, Longman & Todd, Ltd., and Doubleday & Co. Inc., for selected citations from *The Jerusalem Bible*.

Table of Contents

Introduction xi

Chapter One: Gracious God 3
Chapter Two: Holy, Holy, Holy, Lord God! 27
Chapter Three: Merciful God 53
Chapter Four: God's Righteousness 77
Chapter Five: God's Merciful Forgiveness 97
Chapter Six: Jesus, God's Mercy Revealed 117
Chapter Seven: Be Merciful as
Your Father is Merciful 139
Chapter Eight: A World in Need of Mercy 159

Prayer for Mercy 179

GOD'S INCREDIBLE MERCY

Introduction

God's incredible mercy? Yes, it is incredible, too good to believe. God freely loves us, swoops down to our miseries, and forgives us our sins. Scripture attests that his mercy is above all his works. We can count on it through Christ's revelation, which fulfills the Old Testament truth that God will never forsake his children. We are destined by the Trinity to share in the very life of God himself.

And yet how little is written by theologians about God's mercy which is more than just one among many of his attributes. Mercy is that which best describes God's essence. He is condescending and forgiving. His love for us — finite creatures so prone to sin and self-centeredness — is healing and restorative.

When I first thought of writing a book on God's mercy, I checked the libraries of several Catholic universities, all of which offered master and doctoral degrees in theology.

To my surprise I was unable to find a single title on God's mercy. There were many books on God's love. One library had a book dealing with the corporal and spiritual works of mercy that we are supposed to carry out. But not one book on God's mercy!

The Lack Of Mercy In Our Times

POPE JOHN PAUL II, in his beautiful 1980 encyclical on God's Mercy, *Dives in Misericordia*, rightly laments the apparent lack of mercy in the technological countries of the "First World." He claims the reason for this lack is because we so rarely experience true mercy in our individual human relationships and in international relationships among our political leaders. The nuclear powers possess enough force to destroy all life on planet earth many times over. Leaders of nations speak of nuclear "deterrence." Mercy is never mentioned. We live by aggressive violence in the privacy of our hearts, but it manifests itself in our elected officials and their persistence in arms' build up. We increase our defense budgets annually. Meanwhile right in our own affluent society millions are homeless and hungry and deprived of human dignity. Condescending pity is given them, but little compassionate mercy.

God's Mercy Is Above All His Works

ON EVERY PAGE of the Old and New Testaments we read of God's involved, active, condescending and compassionate mercy toward each of us, his children. How beautifully St. Paul summarized the two covenants of the Old and New Testaments: "But . . . God, who is rich in mercy, was moved by the intense love with which he loved us, and when we were dead by reason of our transgressions, he made us live with the life of Christ" (Ep 2:4-5).

The "good news" of God's mercy in all his relations to us, his creatures, is that he does not merely act with mercy, condescending to love us in our brokenness and misery. God *is* mercy! He does not merely act mercifully when we beg Him to show us mercy or give us His forgiveness.

God in His essence is immutable and perfect. Scripture and, above all, the revelation of Jesus Christ, the Word incarnate, show us that when God decreed within the Trinity to create the material world and place man and woman at its center they were to be co-creators of the universe together with him, God also committed himself to give to humankind — freely and with unconditional love — a share in his very own nature (1 Jn 4:8). He bestows his mercy on us in our needs.

What Else But Mercy?

ST. ANTHONY of Egypt, one of the fourth century desert fathers, and the first in a long line of Christian athletes who not only lived in the barren wastelands of the earth, but also in the desert of their hearts, reduced all prayer to mercy. Once asked by other hermits how best to pray, St. Anthony replied: "Hold your hands up to God and pray, 'Have mercy on me!' "

They built their prayer upon God's covenant love (*hesed*) and his promised fidelity (*emet*) in spite of their sinful resistance to his merciful love.

This book represents a "theology of mercy", drawn above all from Scripture and the process theology of the early Christian Fathers of the East. I want to break away from any static, objectivized concept that presents Christian grace and God's holiness and mercy, in terms of acts of God or "things" which He gives to us when we beg for them.

Drawing from the relational language of the early Eastern Fathers who view *grace* primarily as God's uncreated energy of love toward us through all his creation, I realized the first step toward a deeper understanding of divine mercy would be to begin with God as he who is gracious, full of grace, freely, gratuitously, giving himself to us as the triune, personalized community of love.

It is necessary to approach God's mercy by specifying God's gift of himself as grace to us in terms of his holiness. Moving far beyond any static concept of God's holiness as perfection without any self-sacrificing gift to others, I have tried to show God's holiness as his unconditionally, freely-giving gift of himself to us under the aspect of calling us to share in the fellowship of God's very own divine family.

God Is Mercy

UNDERSTANDING GOD'S MERCY in itself, we can comprehend that mercy is not merely and primarily an act of God. Rather, God *is* mercy as he *is* love. God is always "in act" as merciful love toward us in our brokenness and misery. Hence God's mercy is vitally linked to God as *grace* and *holiness*, but in life-giving and unending relationships toward us as God comes into our alienated and sinful condition to heal us and regenerate us by his uncreated energies of love, a love that is first and always merciful.

Another aspect of God's mercy toward us must be considered: God's righteousness. So easily, we presume on God's mercy without the disciplined response to uproot from our lives all elements of selfishness and sin. Although God's mercy guarantees that God will always condescend to us in our sinfulness to heal and forgive us, yet we must realize how God hates sin. It is a contradiction of his holiness. God's mercy demands that He discipline us to draw us away from sin.

God's Merciful Forgiveness

WE EXAMINE then the aspect of God's merciful *forgiveness*. If God is love and mercy by his very nature and in his free and unconditional relationships with his creatures, then God does not begin to show forgiveness only when we do something to merit it. When God comes to us out of his righteousness and his rejection of sin as opposed to his holy, loving nature, we call his active mercy shown to us *forgiveness*.

Jesus Is God's Mercy Enfleshed

THE CRUCIAL CHAPTER on God's mercy that calls the reader to intense study and affective prayer is *Jesus*, God's revealed mercy. The aim of the incarnational, earthly life of Jesus Christ, his sufferrings and his death on the cross and his glorious risen life in his Body, the Church, is to unveil God's infinite mercy. It is especially as the suffering, compassionate, merciful and suffering Servant of Yahweh that Jesus reveals to us God's true nature as merciful love.

From the New Testament we prayerfully ponder how Jesus grew in experiencing the Father's mercy toward himself in his struggles and temptations. In his teachings, especially in his parables on mercy, we hear the Good News of God's infinite, forgiving love toward us. But, above all, as we contemplate Love poured out on the cross out of mercy for us in our inability to heal ourselves of our sinfulness, we come to believe, through the Spirit of the risen Lord, that our sins can be forgiven by such perfect mercy.

The Father truly rejoices and restores all to us, his prodigal children, who cry out for repentance. He is ever-ready to do this because he is always patiently and mercifully awaiting our repentant return to him.

Works Of Mercy

OUR TRANSFORMATION through God's love made flesh for us in Jesus Christ, revealed through His Spirit: this is what Christianity is all about. As we experience God's perfect mercy toward us in our sinfulness, we are healed and made whole by living no longer for ourselvess, but in and for Christ Jesus.

Abiding in him and permitting that he live in us with the Father and his Holy Spirit, we become a good tree, manifested by the fruits of the Spirit (Gal 5:22) which we bring to all our relations with other creatures. Our response to God's active mercy is to be merciful to all other human beings and to all the created world. The corporal and spiritual works of mercy are the rest of how much of God's mercy we have accepted and have transformed by God's Spirit into active mercy in all our relationships. "Blest are they who show mercy: mercy shall be theirs" (Mt 5:7).

The final chapter brings together in summary fashion all that has been covered in the preceding chapters with the theme of the need for mercy in our times. I concluded with a prayer for mercy.

Mercy is seated in the heart and not in the head. May the following pages stimulate you, as the Fathers of the Desert so often insisted, to see all, do all, and treat all with love and mercy. May you go beyond God's justice to experience mercy as the full manifestation of God: the active, uncreated, merciful energy of love. He shows this attribute toward us and every creature as he so mercifully is involved at each moment in his ongoing creation. Since God *is* mercy, the only response we can give is: "Lord, have mercy." And may we also become mercy, mercy in a merciless world that mockingly seeks justice, but without any mercy to guide its quest.

GEORGE A. MALONEY, S.J.

St. Patrick's Novitiate
Midway City, CA

Solemnity of the Mother of God, 1989

Abbreviations

OLD TESTAMENT

Genesis	Gn	Nehemiah	Ne	Baruch	Ba
Exodus	Ex	Tobit	Tb	Ezekiel	Ezk
Leviticus	Lv	Judith	Jdt	Daniel	Dn
Numbers	Nb	Esther	Est	Hosea	Ho
Deuteronomy	Dt	1 Maccabees	1 M	Joel	Jl
Joshua	Jos	2 Maccabees	2 M	Amos	Am
Judges	Jg	Job	Jb	Obadiah	Ob
Ruth	Rt	Psalms	Ps	Jonah	Jon
1 Samuel	1 S	Proverbs	Pr	Micah	Mi
2 Samuel	2 S	Ecclesiastes	Ec	Nahum	Na
1 Kings	1 K	Song of Songs	Sg	Habakkuk	Hab
2 Kings	2 K	Wisdom	Ws	Zephaniah	Zp
1 Chronicles	1 Ch	Sirach	Si	Haggai	Hg
2 Chronicles	2 Ch	Isaiah	Is	Malachi	Ml
Ezra	Ezr	Jeremiah	Jr	Zechariah	Zc
		Lamentations	Lm		

NEW TESTAMENT

Matthew	Mt	Ephesians	Ep	Hebrews	Heb
Mark	Mk	Philippians	Ph	James	Jm
Luke	Lk	Colossians	Col	1 Peter	1 P
John	Jn	1 Thessalonians	1 Th	2 Peter	2 P
Acts	Ac	2 Thessalonians	2 Th	1 John	1 Jn
Romans	Rm	1 Timothy	1 Tm	2 John	2 Jn
1 Corinthians	1 Cor	2 Timothy	2 Tm	3 John	3 Jn
2 Corinthians	2 Cor	Titus	Tt	Jude	Jude
Galatians	Gal	Philemon	Phm	Revelation	Rv

CHAPTER ONE

Gracious God

The basic faith-act that Christians live by is the revelation that "God *is* love" (1 Jn 4:8). Giving and sharing in self-emptying love is not only God's name, but his nature. He does not love as a singular act and then stop loving. He is continually loving so that his very essence as God is always *to be loving.*

We human beings are all made for love, to be loved by God's community of love, the Trinity. We are to be transformed by that consuming fire of divine love and to be love to other human persons. Yet, no word in our English language has been so abused and misunderstood in its true meaning as the word, *love*.

Playboy's understanding of love is centered on the human individual in search of human "objects" to satisfy his sense pleasures. Such love does not go out to discover one's uniqueness in unselfish giving to another, but it turns in on oneself in a sickly way.

So often, we Christians, in our loving relations toward God and other persons, may also conceive love as receiving from, and not as a self-emptying toward, another. In prayer and in the sacraments, we wish to receive from God consolations and a sense of well-being and security from eternal death. Above all, we desire graces to make our lives on earth pleasant and to guarantee a pleasant existence for all eternity.

Idea Of God

WHEN YOU HEAR the word, *love*, what thoughts spring up in your mind? What do you think of when you hear the word, God? How do you habitually understand God in relationship to yourself? Who is God for you?

When it comes to their habitual perception of God, I believe it is fair to say we can divide the majority of Christians into two groups. Those in the first group consider God as monotheistic, an object, the Supreme Being, omnipotent and omniscient. He is perfect and unchangeable. He is essentially good and loving, but he remains far away, locked in his static perfections, without any real, concrete relationships with human individuals in the existential situations of daily living.

To persons of the first group God is somewhat relational, not in himself, but in comparison with our human, weak and sinful nature. He becomes someone who in his omnipotence can give us things so we can be happy, healthy, prosperous, without suffering and thus we can enjoy a guarantee against any form of death in this life. To these individuals, God is only a giving-God.

The other group of Christians, surely a minority, just as the *Anawim*, the *Remnant* people, the poor and lowly of Yahweh who were among the Israelites in the Sinai Desert of the Old Testament, understand God as a community of inter-relating, trinitarian persons. Out of their mutual love for each other, Father and Son, in the bonding love of the Holy Spirit, we human beings have been freely made by the Trinity according to their own "image and likeness" (Gn 1:26).

Such Christians live in the mystery of knowledge given by the Holy Spirit. They experience God as a community of self-giving, loving, divine persons, relating to us just as Jesus Christ, the Word of God made flesh, who images the passionate, concerned love of God for us, especially in His death-resurrection through the Holy Spirit.

God seeks, in the incredible Good News of Jesus Christ, to share his very own nature with us. But his nature is love, love through which God empties himself on our behalf. Totally free, God gratuitously pledges himself to be ever faithful in his self-giving love. He comes to us in our misery and selfishness as compassionate mercy.

God's mercy, Scripture assures us, is above all his works. "He, Yahweh, is merciful, tenderhearted, slow to anger, very loving, and universally kind; Yahweh's tenderness embraces all his creatures" (Ps 145:9). In his relations with his children, God is portrayed consistently in both the Old and New Testaments as He-Who-is-mercy-and-goodness. He swoops down to help those in distress. He is anxious to bring comfort to those in misery. He wishes to deliver them from their infidelity and wretchedness and to transform them into little less than gods (Ps 8:5).

God Is Love

TO UNDERSTAND GOD'S MERCY of healing, compassionate, and faithful love in our miseries, we need to understand more fully that God's very nature is *to be* loving. All God's perfections, especially as he personally relates to us, are manifestations of God-as-love.

God-as-love is the same as God-loving, both within the Trinity and in his loving relationships with us, his creatures. In God's loving relationship with us, we can distinguish theologically, but we should never separate His love from his *grace, holiness, mercy* and *righteousness*. These are not attributes of God so much as they are manifested perfections of God's very essence as love-in-action toward us human beings.

Thus, we must begin with the most primal of all love relationships in which all God's love relationships are grounded: the community of love, the Trinity.

The great 19th-century German theologian, M.J. Scheeben, emphasizes our need for faith — belief given through the Holy Spirit — that is communicated to us through God's revelation in Scripture.

> Without belief in God's revelation it cannot be known at all; and even for believers it is incomprehensible in an exceptionally high degree, indeed, in the highest degree. There it is a mystery in the truest, highest, most beautiful sense of the word (*The Mysteries of Christianity*; p. 48).

God's fullest revelation is made in his incarnate Word, Jesus Christ. In him we have not only words, but *the* one Word, a living person, the Word made flesh Who has dwelt among us (Jn 1:14; Heb 1:1-4). We have no way of knowing the Father and the family of the triune God, except through the revelation made by God's Word, Jesus Christ.

In him we can come, not only to know God's very nature, but to participate in loving communion with God's very being as love. We can become truly sharers of God's very own nature (2 P 1:4).

God Trinity

BY LISTENING to the Word enfleshed for love of us, we can know what the inner life of the Trinity is like. It is through the Word made flesh that we learn of the communitarian sharing within the Trinity, model of the same trinitarian energies of love that are shared with us human beings "outside" of the primal triune community of love. We are caught up in the absolute reality that is at the heart of all other reality, that which is the beginning and the end of all being.

God the Father, the "unoriginated Source of being," in absolute silence and in perfect freedom, in a communication of love impossible for us human beings to understand, speaks his one eternal Word through his Spirit of love. In that one Word, the Father is perfectly present, totally self-giving to His Son: "In him lives the fullness of divinity" (Col 2:9).

In his Spirit, the Father also hears his Word come back to him in a perfect, eternal "yes" of total, surrendering love that is again the same Holy Spirit. The Trinity is a reciprocal community of a movement of the Spirit of love between Father and Son. Our minds cannot fathom the peace and joy, the ardent excitement and exuberant self-surrender that flow in a reposeful motion between Father and Son through the Holy Spirit. God is real only because he communicates in Love with his Word. His Word gives him his identity as Father. That means eternal self-giving to the Other, his Word, in Love. Entering into this trinitarian community of three relational Persons is impossible for us, except through God's revelation: Jesus Christ, the Word of God made flesh.

God's Freedom

TRUE LOVE, as found in the Trinity, consists of *kenotic* loving (cf.: St. Paul's use of this Greek word for *self-emptying* in Ph 2:7), which is a complete gift of oneself to the other. To be both gift and giver, individuals must be free from all outside coercion or force. The gift of self in true love must be completely gratuitous.

These two words, *love* and *freedom*, touch on the basic, awesome mystery of the Trinity, both within intrinsic trinitarian relationships and in extrinsic relationships toward us, God's chosen children. True love and true freedom can never be separated. To love freely is the way God is God. God's being consists in his nature as the One-who-loves in freedom. God exercises his freedom in his-being-love. He exists as free by freely exercising his love.

God As Grace

NOW WE ARE ABLE to begin our journey toward an understanding of God's mercy by seeing

God as grace. In Scripture, grace has many meanings, since it is at the very heart of God's free gift of himself in active relationship with humankind. In general, we must insist, from God's viewpoint, that grace primarily is God in his distinctive mode of actively seeking and creatively sharing a fellowship with us human beings by a free favor which is unconditioned by any work we may do to merit God's favor. God's love is not only considered as a *gracious* gift of himself to us who are totally deserving, but his love cannot be hindered or stopped in any way by our sinful resistance.

Let us, for a moment, examine Scripture's view of *grace*, so different from our usual Western way of viewing it as a created "thing" that we work to merit. As a preface to seeing the various shades of meaning Scripture attaches to the concept of *grace*, we need to recall a basic principle which will allow us to remain in the dynamics of real relationships with the Trinity and, thus, prevent any static view that may present grace as a mere extrinsic object which we come to possess through our own efforts.

St. Paul gives us the setting of God's unconditional, undeserved divine love for us:

> Before the world was made, he chose us, chose us in Christ,
> to be holy and spotless, and to live through love in his presence,
> determining that we should become his adopted sons,
> through Jesus Christ,
> for his own kind purposes,
> to make us praise the glory of his grace,
> his free gift to us in the Beloved,
> in whom, through his blood,
> we gain our freedom,
> the forgiveness of our sins.
> Such is the richness of the grace

which he has showered on us
in all wisdom and insight....
And it is in him that we were claimed as God's own,
chosen from the beginning,
under the predetermined plan of the one
who guides all things as he decides by his own will;
chosen to be,
for his greater glory,
the people who would put their hopes in Christ
before he came (Ep 1:4-12).

Karl Rahner describes well the basic principle which we always need to keep in mind as we ponder the mystery of God's pursuing love in our created order. Rahner describes his theological principle to explain how the Trinity relates with the created world, especially human beings: "The 'economic Trinity' is the 'immanent Trinity' and the 'immanent Trinity' is the 'economic' Trinity" (*The Trinity*, p. 22).

This means that the very free, unconditional activities of the interpersonal relationships of the triune God — Father, Son and Holy Spirit — within the Trinity are the same personalized relationships of Father, Son and Holy Spirit going out of the Trinity toward the historical world of created beings.

There can be no true Christian understanding of *grace*, namely, that grace is primarily God in his free, unconditional giving of himself to the other, unless we perceive the inner activities of the Trinity as the same activities of the Trinity in the mode of *being* toward us human beings. Grace is the mode in which God freely gives himself to us, and this grace flows out of the intrinsic nature of God within the Trinity.

In so doing, both Karl Rahner and the early Eastern Fathers present, as basic to the subject of grace, the personalism of the three Divine Persons in their one "essential" act of self-communication to us human beings. If this were not so, Rahner argues, "God would be the 'giver,' not the gift itself. He would 'give himself' only to the extent that he communicates a gift distinct from himself" (op.cit., p. 101).

One can see why it is so important to approach the topic of *grace* as the mode of God's loving, similar to intrinsic workings within the Trinity and to extrinsic works in the economy of salvation. Otherwise, would we ever be truly saved and set free from our sinfulness and self-centeredness? Only by faith can we have the certainty that we human beings are so freely loved by God that we can become radically transformed by God's gift of himself and by his very own transforming Persons: the Father, the Son and the Holy Spirit. If grace is not primarily God-Trinity freely loving us as our Heavenly Father in his Son, Jesus Christ, through his Spirit, then, we are merely extrinsically "affiliated" with God in a salvation of decree, and not of true "regeneration."

Grace The Uncreated Energy Of Love

SCRIPTURE clearly teaches that God in his essence cannot be known or experienced by us human beings. "Then I will take my hand away and you shall see the back of me; but my face is not to be seen" (Ex 33:23). We can never fully see God or comprehend him as he really is in his essence. "No one has ever seen God" (1 Jn 4:12;

Jn 1:18; 6:46). To understand him as he truly is, we would have to be of the very same nature as God.

Yet, the Good News that Jesus makes possible through his Holy Spirit is that we Christians can truly experience God as self-giving Persons, Father, Son and Holy Spirit. Jesus Christ, through his Holy Spirit, makes it possible for us to "know" God through the Spirit's faith, hope and charity, and to experience God as our loving Father. We can live each moment in the mystery of God's self-emptying love as discovered inside of each event through the uncreated energy of love.

The doctrine of the early Eastern Fathers concerning grace, primarily as the Trinity giving themselves to us as uncreated energies of love, has much to teach us. If we are to live each moment in the mystery of God's gracious love, then we must be able to discover him essentially as one God, loving us with an everlasting, unchanging love as three unique Persons.

The early Eastern Fathers teach us that God, through these energies of love, communicates himself to us in a new knowing and a new participation. These energies are God's mode of existing in relationship to His created world, especially to us human beings, as grace: Divine Giver and Divine Gift, freely bestowed upon us to divinize us into sharers of his very own life.

> But to as many as welcomed him
> he gave the power to become children of God,
> those who believe in his name;
> who were born not of blood,
> or of carnal desire,
> or of man's will;
> no, they were born of God (Jn 1:12-13).

This divine, uncreated energy of love is not a *thing*, an extrinsic "grace" that God heaps upon us in a covering manner. Rather, it is truly God as grace, giving himself to us, his children, as outpoured love in the context of each daily situation.

Through the doctrine of God's energies of love, the Trinity, one in essence and now understood as "God-for-us," we can solve the antinomy between a God Who cannot, in any way, be comprehended in his essence, and a God, as *grace*, freely willing to share himself as Gift in his created children, and Who constantly communicates himself to us through creation. The reason why God created us human beings can only be because God is *grace*, not coerced by any outside force and because God-Trinity wishes to share his divine life by divinizing us into his true children.

> Think of the love that the Father has lavished on us,
> by letting us be called God's children;
> and that is what we are. . . .
> My dear people,
> we are already the children of God,
> but what we are to be in the future has not yet been revealed;
> all we know is, that when it is revealed,
> we shall be like him
> because we shall see him as he really is (1 Jn 3:1-2).

We cannot deny that God gives us created "graces," sanctifying and actual, which can increase and diminish. But in order to understand the mercy and the love of God toward us, we must perceive God as grace in his gratuitous, free-gifting of himself to us in all his energetic actions. Such a scriptural view avoids any static objectivizing of grace as primarily a created accident that we human beings can live without and still be considered truly human beings. St.

Thomas Aquinas, using Aristotle's categories, defines grace as the external principle of human actions. "Man needs a power added to his natural power by grace," wrote Aquinas (*Summa Theologiae*; I; 2nd; Q.109).

What is crucial in our more biblical concept of God as grace is that, through God's energies, we actually are able to make contact with the living God. God is truly love. God is loving-Gift, freely given. Therefore, God is *grace*. God wants to give us (and this is the Good News Jesus brings us), not only created graces, favors and aids in our weaknesses but, above all, he wants to give us himself as Gift. The energy is really the triune God and not a created gift. God gives us himself directly as he is personalized in his energies.

Grace In The Old Testament

LET US TURN to the Bible to grasp more fully the concept of God as grace. In the Old Testament, we find grace presented as a very rich concept at the very heart of God's mode of relating to us human beings. For this reason, several words are used to convey this richness. The Old Testament scholar, Nelson Glueck, in his book: *Hesed in the Bible*, gives an exposition of the main Hebrew words used to express the meaning of grace and mercy: *aheb, hen, hanan,* and *hesed*. We will develop *hesed* in the chapter on mercy. In the Greek Septuagint Old Testament, the word, *charis*, is the word usually used to translate *aheb, hen* and *hanan*.

The Old Testament describes God's freedom in giving us human beings a share in His divine life in terms of a condescending mercy that partakes of very rich and nuanced insights about his freedom and love. *Aheb* is the Hebrew word that expresses God's unconditional love. It reflects nothing of Israel's ability to deserve God's favor, but it flows out of the wonderful, free choice by a living and loving God, willing to share his life with his people. This is seen in the "graceful" text in Deuteronomy:

> If Yahweh set his heart on you and chose you, it was not because you outnumbered other peoples: you were the least of all peoples. It was for love of you . . . that Yahweh brought you out with his mighty hand redeemed you from the house of slavery, from the power of the Pharaoh, king of Egypt. Know then the Yahweh, your God, is God indeed, the faithful God who is true to his covenant and his graciousness for thousand generations. . . . (Dt 7:7-10).

God's graciousness is underlined by the use of the word, *hen*, a noun, which describes the quality in God which arouses the granting of an unmerited favor. *Hanan* is the root verb which means to show favor. The Greek equivalent is the word, *charis*. *Hen* stresses the unmerited quality of God's love for any human person or persons. God's complete freedom, with no obligation to bestow his kind favors, is stressed. Such a gratuitous favor is shown to someone who had petitioned such a favor. God responds in kindness and compassion as he gives aid totally out of his proper nature as being loving grace.

In the Old Testament, we see often that the one seeking God's favor throws him/herself completely upon the good will of God, who is superior and from whom the favor is sought. We could conceive grace as the favor granted, but always in the Old Testament writings the emphasis is on God who *graciously* (full of grace) grants the favor freely and with complete gratuitousness.

In Ps 4:3 we see God granting the favor requested by delivering the psalmist from distress: "Know this, Yahweh works wonders for those he loves, Yahweh hears me when I call him". To "seek God's face" is to cry out for the presence of God as loving deliverer.

> Yahweh, hear my voice as I cry!
> Pity me! Answer me!
> My heart has said of you,
> 'Seek his face'.
> Yahweh, I do seek your face;
> do not hide your face from me (Ps 27:7-9).

Over and over, especially in the Psalms, we find God graciously granting deliverance from distress, which is punishment merited by sin. Such favor is God's forgiveness.

> Have mercy on me, O God, in your goodness,
> in your great tenderness, wipe away my faults,
> wash me clean of my guilt,
> purify me from my sin. . . .
>
> For I am well aware of my faults,
> I have my sin constantly in mind,
> having sinned against none other than you,
> having done what you regard as wrong.
>
> Instill some joy and gladness into me,
> let the bones you have crushed rejoice again.
> Hide your face from my sins,
> wipe out all my fault.
>
> God, create a clean heart in me,
> put into me a new and constant spirit,
> do not banish me from your presence,
> do not deprive me of your holy spirit.

Be my savior again, renew my joy,
keep my spirit steady and willing;
and I shall teach transgressors the way to you,
and to you the sinners will return (Ps 51:1-4, 8-13).

Jesus Christ Is Grace

Charis in the New Testament is the Greek word used to convey the Old Testament concept of God's granting a favor or kindness gratuitously to those in need. St. Paul beautifully expresses Old Testament *hen* when he describes how great is God's grace in Jesus Christ. Here we see the primary meaning of grace linked with God's gift of Jesus who brings us out of sin and death into God's eternal life.

> But God loved us with so much love that he was generous with his mercy: when we were dead through our sins, he brought us to life with Christ — it is through grace that you have been saved — and raised us up with him and gave us a place with him in heaven, in Christ Jesus.
>
> This was to show for all ages to come, through his goodness towards us in Christ Jesus, how infinitely rich he is in grace. Because it is by grace that you have been saved, through faith; not by anything of your own, but by a gift from God; not by anything that you have done, so that nobody can claim the credit. We are God's work of art, created in Christ Jesus to live the good life as from the beginning he had meant us to live it (Ep 2:4-10).

Now all grace is focused in the New Testament upon Jesus Christ, who not only brings us the grace of salvation, but who is the *grace of salvation*; he is God's gift of love sent into our lives to "save" us. The gift of him as our Savior can never be anything other than God's freely outpoured Gift of the Second Person of the Trinity, the Word made flesh who dwelt among us (Jn 1:14).

> So marked, indeed, has been God's love for the world that he gave his only-begotten Son; everyone who believes in him is not to perish, but to have eternal life. The fact is, God did not send the Son into the world to condemn the world. Not at all; the world is to be saved through him. He who believes in him is not liable to condemnation, whereas he who refuses to believe is already condemned, simply because he has refused to believe in the name of the only-begotten Son of God (Jn 3:16-18).

Grace Given Through The Holy Spirit

ST. JOHN THE EVANGELIST clearly shows us in his *Prologue* that it is in Jesus that the fullness of God's grace has come to us. "And of his fullness we have all received a share — yes, grace succeeding grace; for the Law was granted through Moses, but grace and truth have come through Jesus Christ" (Jn 1:16-17). Yet, St. Paul teaches us that "No one can say, 'Jesus is Lord' unless he is under the influence of the Holy Spirit" (1 Col 12:3). The Spirit leads us into the whole truth of the Gospel (Jn 16:13). He convinces us of the truth that Jesus is "the Way, the Truth and the Life" (Jn 14:6). He allows us to enter into a union with Christ as closely as branches are an integral part of a vine (Jn 15:1) in order to bring forth great fruits of love toward others.

In the New Testament, we see that we cannot experience God's freeing love, his *grace* as the mode by which he freely and unconditionally gives himself to us in our sinfulness, except through the power of the Holy Spirit given to us through the risen Jesus. The Spirit gives us the power that he gave to Jesus, the first-born Son of the Father, to say always, "Abba, Father" (Rm 8:15; Gal 4:6), and to know we are no longer slaves, but freed children of God. It is the Spirit who prays within us (Rm 8:26-27) to reveal to our consciousness through faith, hope and love that Jesus *is* God's grace who freely loves us in our oppression and sets us free by allowing us to commit ourselves totally to Jesus as Lord.

Through the Spirit, we know that Jesus *is* grace, the Image of the Father, acting out in human form, especially on the cross, and now through his resurrectional presence dwelling within us, that God has granted us a share with Jesus in his inheritance, which brings freedom for those whom God has taken for his own to make his glory praised (Ep 1:13-14). The Spirit's primary function is to create in us the new life of God in Christ Jesus.

Redeeming Grace

WE SEE in the New Testament that Jesus is most manifested as God's grace to us when he images the free gift of God unto his death on the cross. Nowhere in all of Scripture do we look up and contemplate the mystery of God as *grace* so dramatically as when we look upon the face of God in the Suffering Servant of Yahweh, Jesus, hanging on the cross and poured out to the last drop of water and blood on our behalf!

Knowing through the Holy Spirit that Jesus is the expressed Image of the Heavenly Father and is God's gracious, free gift of love, totally given to us through his death on the cross, we can rejoice in Jesus as God's redeeming *grace*. As we look upon Love poured out freely for us, we see *grace* as God's free turning toward us, his creatures, as perfect Gift of love. We see our own unworthiness through God's infinite transcendence. Through the Spirit, we believe only perfect transcendence of God makes possible His humble, gratuitous condescension by the Gift of himself in complete self-emptying love.

We realize that we have no claim on such a loving sacrifice, such a gracious Gift in Jesus. This is always the negative aspect of grace. It can never be due to any work, or anything we can offer to God, in order to merit it. We cannot condition God's Gift of Himself Who is free *grace*. This is what is meant that the Lord is *gracious* and merciful (Ps 144:8). His coming down to our darkened level of sin and death in Jesus Christ is free and unconditional on God's part.

Grace As Forgiveness Of Sins

THE BIBLICAL CONCEPT of grace is never seen in any abstract theologizing about its objective characteristics. We see the qualities of grace discovered in the dialogue between God and sinful human beings. God is all-holy, unconditionally loving, with a love that condescends in self-emptying love to the level of us resisting human beings. He gives himself unto death. We either accept his Gift of love or reject it through the idolatry of continued sin.

Thus, we need the negative quality of grace, as we have pointed out, since we are totally unworthy of God's condescending love. We are, in the words of St. Irenaeus of the second century, nothing but "empty receptacles to be filled by God's goodness." We are, even before our creation, included in God's designs and predestined by His eternal grace. But we have also been born into sin, so that with St. Paul we must all admit that even now there is sin in our members (Rm 7:24).

We were meant by God's grace to be happy children of our one Heavenly Father. We were to live in oneness and harmony with all other human beings as brothers and sisters of a large family. The birds and animals, the stars and sun, the waters and the inhabitants of the sea, the earth and its produce were meant to be harnessed by us into a joyful yielding to help all persons grow into greater love and happiness.

But, from the first moment of our birth until this present moment, we look around and see ourselves sitting like very disturbed children in isolated corners: sick, lonely, angry and shivering with fears. We have forgotten how to communicate with God. We speak to our neighbors in a monologue of noisy silence. Materialism has dried up our hearts and strewn the arid desert with tinsel and baubles, leaving us like discarded Christmas trees on a dump heap.

Truly we feel sin within us and around us. Sin, as in the Old Testament, is anything which deliberately or indeliberately, regardless of the cause, is an obstacle preventing us from accepting God's grace. We feel caught in a prison of darkness, and yet we have no power to even hope for help from a loving God, unless God calls us.

Our resistance, however, does not prevent God from being gracious toward us. Sin is our history. We have not only inherited the sin of Adam, but we have added to that sin by our own sinful willfulness. But, St. Paul assures us that God, as grace, does overcome our sin, if we wish to accept his loving condescension to our brokenness.

> If it is certain that through one man's fall so many died, it is even more certain that divine grace, coming through the one man, Jesus Christ, came to so many as an abundant free gift.... If it is certain that death reigned over everyone as the consequence of one man's fall, it is even more certain that one man, Jesus Christ, will cause everyone to reign in life who receives the free gift that he does not deserve, of being made righteous (Rm 5:15, 17).

This forgiving grace is not an attribute of God's nature that flashes across the darkened sky like a bolt of lightning on a hot summer night, only to leave the sky and the world still covered with darkness. God *is* grace as his habitual mode of manifesting himself as God, as divine, as the triune community of perfect love and holiness toward us.

God does not begin to call us to his grace and righteousness. It is we who must accept his nature as eternally gracious toward us. The prophet Joel dramatically has Yahweh call us to his grace by repentance. Yet, even this act of acceptance is a part of God's initial gift of who he is as God:

> Come back to me with all your heart,
> fasting, weeping, mourning.
> Let your hearts be broken, not your garments torn,
> turn to Yahweh your God again,
> for he is all tenderness and compassion,
> slow to anger, rich in graciousness,
> and ready to relent (Jl 2:12-13).

Acceptance Of God's Grace

EVEN WHEN WE in our brokenness resolve to rise and go back to our heavenly Father and receive his reconciliation and forgiveness (Lk 15:17-18), God's operative grace has always been there, especially through the workings of the Spirit of love. Repentance is our desire to accept what has always been present in our lives, namely, that God's grace is of the very essence of God's being God as condescending and forgiving love.

We cannot buy God's grace by any feats of repentance or of heroic penances endured out of sorrow for our sins. In a word, we receive it through no merit of our own. It is freely present as the very essence of God, gracious, tender and compassionate, as love always emptying out toward us as he gifts us with himself.

What assurance our faith in God's revelation must give us that he does truly forgive us our sins! There can be no doubt or uncertainty that God forgives us our sins and restores us to oneness with Christ as heirs of Heaven (Rm 8:17).

> Yahweh is tender and compassionate,
> slow to anger, most loving,
> his indignation does not last forever,
> his resentment exists a short time only;
> he never treats us, never punishes us,
> as our guilt and our sins deserve (Ps 103:8-10).

St. Paul understands, so clearly, that nothing but God's goodness and holiness wipe away our sins forever and bring us into a sharing of God's own holiness and love. "Both Jew and pagan sinned and forfeited God's glory, and both are justified through the free gift of his grace by being redeemed in Christ Jesus who was appointed by God to sacrifice his life so as to win reconciliation through faith" (Rm 3:24-25).

Again, Paul clearly shows us the complete gratuitous gift of redemption in the grace that Jesus is: ". . . It was not because he was concerned with any righteous actions we might have done ourselves; it was for no reason except his own compassion that he saved us, by means of the cleansing water of rebirth and by renewing us with the Holy Spirit which he has so generously poured over us through Jesus Christ, our savior. He did this so that we should be justified by his grace, to become heirs looking forward to inheriting eternal life" (Tt 3:5-8).

Accepting Love In Action

IT IS GOD'S GRACE through Christ Jesus which attacks sin in us at the root. By God's presence as love — full of graciousness and tenderness and mercy — all our fears, guilt and self-centeredness are transformed just as the morning dawn dissipates the darkness of night. When we accept God's love in action, we experience God as grace. There is no other way we can turn from the state of no-grace to fullness-of-grace than to accept God as *grace*.

God acts, ultimately, as love in action toward us only because God is, by his nature, grace that acts graciously within the Trinity for all eternity.

We can, therefore, summarize that grace is not primarily an extrinsic manifestation of God in his created gifts, even though he does give us "created graces." But, such graces would never exist, unless God is, by his very nature, grace itself. This is a mystery that can be accepted only by faith.

In the Trinity, there is no special condescension between the Father and Son toward the Spirit. There can be no opposition or resistance through self-centeredness that needs to be overcome. Within the Trinity, there is grace as pure love, agapic love, that is self-emptying in order to live for the Other. It is *kenosis*, or grace in its purest form of humble, self-emptying that the other may live. It is total availability in perfect mutuality or equality of one and the same nature along with purest self-sacrifice for the other.

From this divine Source alone, the Trinity, God, as grace, created us freely, unconditionally and, condescendingly, turns toward his children in their miseries. Gracefully and graciously the triune God lures us out of our sinfulness by overcoming our resistance sheerly by his love as self-sacrificing grace.

With joyful exultation, God whispers in the excitement of himself accepted by us his creatures, as grace poured out:

> "Welcome, my child! You are dead and have now come back to life! You were lost and now have been found! . . . And they began to celebrate" (Lk 15:24).

CHAPTER TWO

Holy, Holy, Holy, Lord God

Today, many schools of psychology, which follow the ideas of Abraham Maslow and Carl Rogers, speak of *authenticity* in the development of the integrated human person. The younger generation insists, "I must be authentic, real, *myself!*"

What would it mean if God were to reveal himself in all his unique authenticity? What is God deep down in the essence of his divinity? Scripture, especially the Old Testament, over and over, describes God as *holy*. In order to prepare for our theme of God's mercy, we need to explore this important characteristic of God as *holiness*. This topic will have vital meaning for describing our true selves, created according to God's image and likeness, Jesus Christ.

In the First Epistle of Peter we see our human goal revealed to us: to be holy as God is holy. ". . . Be holy in all you do, since it is the Holy One who has called you"; and Scripture says: "Be holy, for I am holy" (1 P 1:15-16).

In Scripture, whenever God is described as holy, he is always close to human beings or angels, involved in communicating his loving nature so that his perfection may be shared in a union of love.

> For it is I, Yahweh, who am your God. You have been sanctified and have become holy because I am holy.... Yes it is I, Yahweh, who have brought you out of Egypt to be your God; you, therefore, must be holy because I am holy (Lv 11:44-45).

Grace And Holiness

IN ORDER to reach the essence of God's mercy, we need to discover what God's holiness means. Let us first see how grace and holiness are interrelated. We have seen how God as *grace* is God, in the fullness of his nature, loving gratuitously. With complete freedom, he gives himself to us in our absolute unworthiness to receive such a gift. We saw that, not only creatureliness, but, also, our sinful resistance to close ourselves off from God as free Gift, does not diminish God's continued pursuing us and gifting us with himself.

It is we human beings in our finite understanding of God's perfection who need to qualify and expand the concentrated concept of God as gracious love. Therefore, holiness of God does not change what we have already said about grace. Holiness highlights for us, and prepares us to understand the rich concept of God as mercy toward us by positing God in his "wholly otherness" to us. We will see him as totally distinct from us. His way of loving us is completely different from the way other intellectual beings, angelic or human, love.

The concept of holiness amplifies the notion of grace, as it presents to us in Scripture, God, as willingly and freely seeking actively to create with us a loving community, a *koinonia*, or friendship in the Spirit of love, so that we can truly participate in his very nature. Yet, this loving union through the holiness of God prevents us from dissolving God and ourselves into a unity without any uniqueness or distinction of God, or even of ourselves.

Far Eastern religions, especially Hinduism and Buddhism, stress the mystical union between God the Absolute and us human beings without maintaining the absolute transcendence of God, in his being true to himself in all his actions toward us. "New Age" thinking, also, succumbs to a union between human beings and the Ultimate, without any "holiness" left to the reality of God, without any transcendence to God's uniqueness as perfect love.

Christianity insists on the oneness of creatures in God, but holiness preserves also the *otherness* of God, which permits true and even passionate love on the part of God toward his children. Holiness is the special way God's graciousness and perfect freedom come to us through his specifically unique and constant energies of love. Holiness adds a most important dimension to God's essence, not presented in the concept of God as grace. That is, that God in his authenticity in being true to His divine nature as love must, also, judge and abhor anything that resists and opposes himself as grace. God's holiness necessitates that God's will always prevail and this necessitates judgment on what resists God's free love.

God Is Wholly Other

THE PROPHET ISAIAH presents us with his vision in which he beholds God's wholly otherness in his awesome transcendence that separates him from all other beings as Source of all creatures and fullness of *being*. Isaiah is swept up in vision before the throne of God and sees how the Seraphs covered their faces and feet and cry out constantly:

> 'Holy, holy, holy is Yahweh Sabaoth.
> His glory fills the whole earth.'
> The foundations of the threshold shook
> with the voice of the one who cried out,
> and the Temple was filled with smoke.
> I said: 'What a wretched state I am in!
> I am lost, for I am a man of unclean lips
> and I live among a people of unclean lips,
> and my eyes have looked at the King, Yahweh Sabaoth'
> (Is 6:3-5).

Isaiah is not recounting his sins, but rather is experiencing what it means to encounter the absolute transcendence of God as the fullness of *being*. There comes over the prophet a holy fear that fills him with a shuddering and anxiety that the power of God could destroy him in his nothingness and unworthiness to stand before total *being*.

Moses also fell back before the holiness of Yahweh in his encounter with God in the burning bush. For that was *holy* ground (Ex 3:4-6), because God, who is holy, made himself present in that place. No human being could touch the Ark of the Covenant because God's holy presence was in that place. His holiness was localized in the Inner Sanctum, the Holy of Holies, for it was there Yahweh promised to enter into his special loving communication with his people.

Mysterium Tremendum

RUDOLF OTTO, in his book, *The Idea of the Holy*, argues that the experience of God is qualitatively unique and describes it variously as experience of the "numinous," the "holy," the "other." Such an experience brings one forcibly in contact with the Source of all being, of all reality. This Someone is so separate from his creatures, so great, so powerful, that one is, at least initially, unable to assimilate the experience in ordinary ways.

One experiences the "other," first, as *mysterium tremendum*, a "dreadful, shaking, awesome, fearful" mysterious encounter with God whom we cannot control by any force within us. The dread results from an awareness of the object of the experience as something totally other, incomprehensible and powerful.

The effect on any human being encountering God as holy transcendence, as wholly other, is to give that person a lively sense of his/her ontological unworthiness, as we see in Isaiah's vision.

Mysterium Fascinans

YET, the paradox of God's holiness is that, although the experience of his transcendence is dreadful, he seemingly draws us with an inner fascination on our part to reach out and possess him in loving union. So, without the fear filling us with fright and a flight away from this awesome God, we are inevitably drawn into a tender intimacy with God. We wait in "awe-full" reverence for God to reveal more of himself to us. Humility, reverence and a gentle spirit cover us and give us an open receptivity to God's initiative.

This fear of God is found often on the pages of the Old Testament. It is a rich and complex concept that is different from our ordinary experience of being afraid. Psalm 33 best describes this fear that is mingled with hope, God's very transcendence is his desire to bring about an immanent union with himself and his children. God's righteousness is judgment on our resistance to his love. Holiness also brings us in hope to a gracious, self-sacrificing God as Gift.

> But see how the eye of Yahweh is on those who fear him,
> on those who rely on his love,
> to rescue their souls from death
> and keep them alive in famine (Ps 33:18-19).

The prophet Daniel tells that he was so overcome by the awareness of his worthlessness that he trembled, even to the point of fainting. And, yet, he was fascinated and showed a humble willingness to offer himself, even though he realized how unworthy he was, to the "other" (Dn 10).

Holiness In The Old Testament

THE BASIC HEBREW WORD used in the Old Testament to describe God's holiness is *kadosh*. It fundamentally means a "separation." This is the first element grasped in the early understanding of God's holiness in the Old Testament. We have already touched on this aspect of the wholly otherness of God in comparison with the imperfections of his creatures (cf.: Gn 28:10-19; 1 Kg 6:13-21; 2 Kg 6:1-10; Num 4:20).

The response that God's holiness, as utterly other in his transcendence, calls up on the part of human beings is a fear, even to the point of terror (cf.: Ex 3:1-6; Gn 15:12). In the abyss that separates God from his creatures, man and woman understand themselves in their sinfulness and nonauthenticity, in their fragmentation.

The idea of God's holiness, also, takes on the aspect of God, who sanctifies his creatures by giving them his demands as signs of their living in harmony with God's very own nature, as the Absolute Source of all being, who can in righteousness demand a return of love for perfect love given (cf.: Is 12:6; 29:19-23; 30:11-15; 31:1-3; 41:9-14).

Yahweh demonstrates his holiness through his righteousness. ". . . Yahweh Sabaoth will increase his glory by his sentence, the holy God will display his holiness by his integrity" (Is 5:16). God shows his abhorrence of any human moral evil and, thus, reveals his holiness in a way that we find difficult to understand. His holiness is shown by his judgment upon sin. "These are the waters of Meribah, where the sons of Israel challenged Yahweh and he proclaimed his holiness" (Nb 20:13; cf.: Ezk 38:16).

Yahweh executes his righteousness and judgment in a way that is in harmony with his nature as love. As his love and mercy endure forever, Yahweh, in all his actions toward individuals and his chosen people, acts out of his salvific will to deliver his children from their infidelity and idolatry in worshipping their own ego. The prophet Ezekiel combines God's holiness with his wrath upon the sins of his people:

> Sidon, now I set myself against you;
> I will show my glory through you.
> Men shall learn that I am Yahweh,
> since I will execute sentence on her
> and display my holiness in her.
> I will send the plague to her;
> blood shall flow in her streets,
> and in her the dead will fall
> under the sword raised against her on all sides,
> and so men will learn that I am Yahweh (Ezk 28:22).

Yahweh shows his holiness in his judgment upon sin that is always a part of God's consistent willing to share His covenant-love with others whom He has freely chosen. This is aimed at deliverance from sin or redemption. We have seen how God's holiness separates God from all creatures. Yet, in his separateness, he freely wills to bring us into his separateness, giving us a share in his holiness, as we receive his forgiving love for our sinfulness and, then, live in obedience to his commands. "You must keep my commands and put them into practice. I am Yahweh. You must not profane my holy name, so that I may be proclaimed holy among the sons of Israel, I, Yahweh, who sanctify you. I, who brought you out of the land of Egypt to be your God, I am Yahweh" (Lv 22:31-32).

Yahweh shows his holiness in restoring the House of Israel by establishing an order in which his moral law will be supreme and His power over the forces of evil is asserted (cf.: Is 29:23; 41:14; 43:3; Ezk 20:41; 36:23; 39:27).

The Holy One Of Israel

ISAIAH CREATED this title and applied it to Yahweh in his loving relationship with his people, Israel. We find more than twenty-six texts in Isaiah that describe the name of God, or the person of God, as holy in reference always to God's holy actions toward his chosen ones.

God, by his holiness, is separated from the entire created world. But he freely, in his holiness, calls his people to enter into his separation, by the paradox of overcoming any separation in the gift of God's very being with their being. Yet, God calls his chosen ones to leave the world of sin and darkness and to be holy as he is holy. He sanctifies us by redeeming us from all sin and lifts us up to share in his essence as holy.

Isaiah beautifully expresses this in the words he has Yahweh speak through him to his people:

> Do not be afraid, for I have redeemed you;
> I have called you by your name, you are mine.
> Should you pass through the sea, I will be with you;
> or through rivers, they will not swallow you up.
> Should you walk through fire, you will not be scorched
> and the flames will not burn you.
> For I am Yahweh, your God,
> the Holy One of Israel, your savior.
>
> I give Egypt for your ransom,
> and exchange Cush and Seba for you.
> Because you are precious in my eyes,
> because you are honored and I love you,

I give men in exchange for you,
peoples in return for your life.
Do not be afraid, for I am with you (Is 43:1-5).

God's Holiness Made Flesh

WE HAVE SEEN God's holiness revealed over and over in the Old Testament as God in his absolute transcendence that separates him completely from his creatures. Yet God in his "wholly otherness" condescends to pursue his freely chosen people. God's holiness essentially seeks to create a fellowship with his children, a sharing in God's community of self-sacrificing love. Still, such humble, emptying love demands also God's righteousness, as he despises sin and any form of idolatry that would place creatures above himself. God's holiness demands a "tough love," if it is to be true to God's own nature. God chastises his people when they sin because he loves them, but he must despise their sins which prevent them from accepting his call to share in his very own life.

Yet, such holiness in the Old Testament remains hidden to the eyes of his chosen ones. It is revealed by God through the medium of the prophets. Now we turn to the Good News of the New Covenant. Nowhere in God's dealings with his human children has his holiness been more perfectly manifested to us than when his divine Word became flesh. "He is the image of the unseen God" (Col 1:15). Whoever would see him, Jesus Christ, would see the Father (Jn 14:9).

Jesus Holy

GOD HAS CALLED US to be holy as he is holy. But we have no way of experiencing the fullness of God's holiness except in God's Word made flesh, Jesus Christ. Jesus, true wisdom, teaches us about God's holiness. He speaks to us of a concerned Father who seeks in all the details of our daily existence to establish us in his holiness as sharers in the triune community of love.

More importantly, Jesus comes to act out God's holiness. Now we know the answer to the question: What is God's holiness like? It is like the holiness of Jesus. The holiness of Jesus consisted in his having been anointed and sanctified by the Holy Spirit and sent as the gift of the Father through the Spirit to us. He is the holiness of the Father given to us so that we might also become holy, as he is holy, with him through his same Holy Spirit.

All that Jesus had came to him from the Father. He could do nothing of himself, but only what he receives from his Father (Jn 5:19, 30; Jn 8:28). It is the Father who sent him into the world, consecrated him and made him holy in order to bring God's holiness to us (Jn 10:36).

Yet, Jesus, as man throughout his earthly life, in cooperation with the Holy Spirit, had to strive to become holy. In the Last Supper Discourse, Jesus prays to his Father:

> As you sent me into the world,
> I have sent them into the world,
> and for their sake I consecrate myself,
> so that they too may be consecrated in truth (Jn 17:18).

He was driven into the desert by the Holy Spirit (Mk 1:12) and there he was tempted. He was tempted throughout his earthly life, yet remained without sin (Heb 4:15; I Jn 4:15). Jesus was sinless because he yielded to God's Spirit within him and went against any urge of disobedience to the Father's will. He truly became holy as he strove in each moment to do, not his will, but the will of the Father.

The holiness of Jesus is seen, not only as the presence of the Father's Spirit in the Son of Man, giving him strength to unmask and defeat the devil, but also as a growing process, which brings holiness as he confronts the evil one and conquers him.

Through Temptations To Holiness

THE GOSPELS PRESENT the peak of Jesus' holiness as an *exodus* experience. He was tempted in his growth in holiness to hold on to his own life, rather than to surrender it on behalf of sinful mankind. Imaging the Father's holiness in his own human development, Jesus grew in each event as he sought to do, not his own, but his Father's will. "Here I am! I am coming to obey your will" (Heb 10:9).

Jesus saw that certain ways of acting were in perfect harmony with his Father's commands and these he freely carried out, even when this meant his death on the cross (Lk 22:42). His holiness prompted him to a joyful response in carrying out all that his human consciousness revealed to him as compatible with the Father's design or, even more sensitively, what would please his Father more. Jesus could say that his holiness always drove him to "do what pleases him" (Jn 8:29).

It is the terrifying abandonment by his loving Father, while he hung on the cross dying, that becomes for Jesus his last and greatest temptation (Mk 15:34). Unlike the surrender of himself in the desert and in the Garden of Gethsemane where he is consoled by the Father's presence through an angel, on the cross abandonment yielded to total darkness.

Jesus, who had tasted the joys of loving his Father, tasted only a seeming hostility of the Father toward him. Paul explains "For our sake God made the sinless one into sin" (2 Cor 5:21). Here do the love and holiness of Jesus for his Father shine forth in darkness. Light becomes darkness. Holiness becomes sin for our sake. Jesus on the cross, although the holy one of God, freely took on the supreme sacrifice of his life, in order that we might believe in the passionate desire of God-Trinity to share the divine life and their persons with us in loving communion. For this reason, the Father did not spare his Son, but gave him up for all of us (Rm 8:32; Ac 2:23).

Here we see, also, not only God's love for us, but his righteousness played out in terms of suffering to overcome sin. God abhors sin and Jesus acts out this element at the heart of God's essence. As Jesus felt a seeming abandonment by the Father, he who has become one of us in our common sinfulness out of love for us, struggled to remain faithful to the Father. Holiness is ultimately total surrender to God, even if God seemingly rejects the gift.

In spite of his temptations, Jesus pushed to new depths of holiness and loving surrender as he cried our: "Father!" He still gave himself as gift even though the Father did not seem present to receive it. In that struggle Jesus attained, in his human expression, the very holiness of God. This is the victory of his holiness and it is the crowning in human language of the Trinity's holiness, of self-giving to mankind unto death and total abandonment.

Jesus' true holiness came from humiliation unto exaltation, as St. Paul so powerfully presents:

> ... He was humbler yet,
> even to accepting death,
> death on a cross.
> But God raised him high
> and gave him the name
> which is above all other names
> so that all beings
> in the heavens, on earth and in the underworld,
> should bend the knee at the name of Jesus
> and that every tongue should acclaim
> Jesus Christ as Lord
> to the glory of God the Father (Ph 2:8-11).

Holy Through God's Spirit

IF JESUS, through the Holy Spirit, is glorified by the Father and is able to bestow his sanctifying Spirit in his final sufferings upon his believers, it is no less, also, the Holy Spirit who effects the holiness of Jesus at each state of his human development. We see this in his baptism in the Jordan by St. John the Baptist. Jesus sees the Spirit descending upon him as a gentle dove, and he hears his Father declare from on high: "You are my Son, the Beloved, my favor rests on you" (Mk 1:11).

The heavens opened and Jesus is aware in his human consciousness that he is hearing his Heavenly Father and seeing the Holy Spirit come upon him as the Father's gift to him. Deep down, the human Jesus is swept up into an ecstatic oneness with the Father through the Spirit. Like the water that falls down over his human body, so the love of the Father for him, his beloved Son, cascades over him and covers him with glory.

Heaven and earth had been closed by man's first sin in Eden. Now God's communicating presence has passed through the barrier of sin and Jesus, God's holiness, stands within the human family. Light and darkness are brought together in Jesus. By his holiness, we can be reconciled to the Father and be healed of our guilt and sin. Through his death he proves how worthwhile and of what value we are in the sight of the infinite God.

It is the Holy Spirit, the personalized, activating love of the Father toward his son and of the Son toward his Father, who is present, gently reconciling the darkness with the soft breaking of the dawn of a new age. The Spirit brings Jesus, not in this one moment of his baptism, but in every moment of his human existence to a greater, joyful and peaceful assurance that the Father loves him. The Spirit gives Jesus the determination "to be perfect as the Heavenly Father is perfect" (Mt 5:48) and the loving power of fulfilling that desire in all events.

Jesus Most Human

THE PRESENCE AND SANCTIFYING ACTION of the Holy Spirit in the life of Jesus begins with Jesus in his humanity. If St. Paul could appeal to the Corinthians' inner dignity because their bodies were holy: "Your body, you know, is the temple of the Holy Spirit" (1 Cor 6:19), how much more was this a living experience of

Jesus in his human, material body? Jesus not only found the Father working in nature all about him, in the fields, the sea, the sky, the changes of the seasons, the variety of plant and animal life but, also, he continually discovered the Father in the very workings of his own body, indwelling and working to make him holy as the Father is holy.

The Spirit in Jesus allowed Him to grow "in wisdom, in stature, and in favor with God and men" (Lk 2:52). All anxiety was removed from his openness to meet his loving Father in each fresh moment. The situation was not objectivized as either holy or profane for Jesus. But through the inner presence of the Spirit, he moved freely through life's events and circumstances to respond fully according to the Father's mind. Each moment of his life, as he, in his free choices, cooperated with the Father that moment, brought him into a growing experience that in all things he was the Word, one with the mind of the Father. Free from sin and self-seeking, Jesus was free to be loved infinitely by his Father and to strive to respond joyfully in a return of that love.

Love and holiness cannot be separated. It is Jesus' consciousness of the Father's presence within him, dwelling at the core of his being, that makes it possible for Jesus to experience the perfect holiness of his Father. Awareness of the perfect indwelling of the Father, as Jesus affirmed, "I and the Father are one" (Jn 17:22), brought the most intimate union possible, where two become one through self-emptying love for the other.

Thus, in all the human situations experienced by Jesus, he encountered the indwelling presence of the Father and Holy Spirit as outpoured love for him. This freed him from the temptation to live in any way other than what would be a perfect reflection of the Father's holiness.

Jesus Poor

THE HOLINESS OF JESUS reflected itself in all his human relationships, as well as his attitude toward all of God's creatures. We cannot understand Jesus in his personal poverty and his preference for the physically, psychologically, and spiritually poor persons whom he met and to whom he ministered his healing, unless we enter into the conscious relationship that Jesus entered into as the imaged Word of the Father. His basic experience of God's love for mankind was that from man's side there reigned absolute poverty. Man and woman are most radically and ontologically non-entity, except for God's outpoured love in unselfish creation. God is absolute love (*agape*) because he is perfectly holy and self-giving.

As Jesus experienced through the Spirit the riches of God in his holiness poured out into his humanity, he lived "poverty." Such poverty became for him a humble recognition of God's sovereignty and free gift of his love. It was a permanent attitude that Jesus assumed toward himself, his Father, and each person he met. It was poverty that can be called *humility*: Jesus was nothing; the Father was all. He is meek and humble of heart (Mt 11:29). Jesus understood the words of Yahweh in Isaiah: "I live in a high and holy place, but I am ... with the contrite and humbled spirit, to give the humble spirit new life, to revive contrite hearts" (Is 57:15).

Jesus lived poorly because he lived only by the inner richness of his Father's holiness as a continued gift of himself to his eternal Son. He was absolutely poor because no *thing* possessed him. He was possessed only by his Father and so he used things only as an external expression of that inner emptiness before the Allness of his Father.

"Remember how generous the Lord Jesus was; he was rich, but he became poor for your sake, to make you rich out of his poverty" (2 Cor 8:9).

Jesus Serves

JESUS, poor, humble and loving, shows forth all of these characteristics of his holiness which reflects the invisible Heavenly Father by his service toward others. Jesus came to serve because that is love in action and he was acting out, in a human way, the love of the Father.

Whatever God sanctifies, he does so to image his holiness which is love in humble service to build a community of love through self-sacrifice. Jesus knew that true holiness and selfishness, holiness and self-absorption through inactivity, holiness and laziness, are utterly irreconcilable.

Holiness as we see in God's uncreated energies, working for us throughout God's creation, cannot be separated from active, loving service. The more holiness, the greater the fitness for self-giving in service. Jesus understood that the more there is of true holiness, the more there is of God, since God's holiness consists in his desire to share his very being as Gift to his Son.

But, above all, Jesus taught and lived the principle that true concern about the least (Mt 25), in humble service, is essential to true holiness. Anything else would be a holiness that is selfish, which is contradictory, since it is not true love in self-giving.

Jesus, therefore, lived a life of total self-denial and obedience to his Father. Thus, he went forth with total availability, giving himself to each person as he experienced his Father doing to himself and all his human brothers and sisters. The Father's compassion for his children drove Jesus to act out in human expression that same compassion. He never sought his own comfort when others needed him. He burned with an inner fire to actualize the presence of the Father in the lives of all persons whom he met. "I have come to bring fire to the earth, and how I wish it were blazing already" (Lk 12:49).

Jesus serves others most, not only by preaching about the Father's love and holiness but, also, by acting out such holiness. Throughout his entire life, Jesus went about doing good, especially in the form of healing all types of sicknesses and diseases. He was never more the perfect image of the Father's holiness than when he saw the multitudes fainting and scattered abroad as sheep without a shepherd, and he was moved with mercy and compassion (Mt 9:36).

Jesus shows us his holiness and the imaged holiness of his Father in his self-giving to each individual who had a need. He lives to remove from human lives any pain or suffering and to replace it with exuberant, rich, happy health and fulfillment, and to bring a more abundant life (Jn 10:10). Jesus' service to those in need is love enacted, even unto death. No greater loving service or holiness does a human being (or God himself) have than to lay down his life for a friend (Jn 15:13).

Jesus Is Love

JESUS is holy as his Heavenly Father is holy because, in a word, he is filled with the Father's love, the Holy Spirit. All other characteristics of his holiness are summarized in the one phrase: Jesus *is* love. The love of God conquers in him at the peak of his filial obedience to the Father in dying on our behalf. He is holy by being one with God's holiness, Yet, Jesus shows us that in his human consciousness he grows into greater holiness as he gives up his will in order, lovingly, to do his Father's will. Holiness is ultimately the will to live totally for the other, to become the "slave" by the gift of oneself, to lovingly serve the other.

Jesus becomes God's holy Word in his complete obedience unto death (Ph 2:8). As he became holy by learning obedience, so we must also:

> Although he was Son, he learnt to obey through suffering; but having been made perfect, he became for all who obey him, the source of eternal salvation and was acclaimed by God with the title of high priest of the order of Melchizedek (Heb 5:8-10).

Be Holy As I Am Holy

AS JESUS COULD SAY: "As the Father has loved me, so I have loved you" (Jn 15:9), so also he could say to you and me: "As I am holy because my Father is holy, so you also be holy as I am holy to you." Jesus' formula whereby we, his followers, can be holy is simple:

> Remain in my love.
> If you keep my commandments,
> you will remain in my love,
> just as I have kept my Father's commandments
> and remain in his love. . . .
> This is my commandment:
> love one another,
> as I have loved you (Jn 15:9-12).

Thus, Jesus teaches us that the link between our redemption and holiness is the degree of our response in obedience to obey Jesus' commands to love God with our whole heart and love our neighbor as he has loved us. We reveal whether we are holy as Jesus by the fruit we bring forth. Only actions prove our faith-response in holiness and show the degree of our holiness in concrete obedience, love and surrender within the context of each human situation.

Holiness, therefore, is not only God's gift of himself in order that we can, through Jesus and his Spirit, live in God's community, but it is also an acquirement on our part. Jesus shows the way and through his sanctifying Spirit gives us the power to become holy as he is. Jesus is "the radiant light of God's glory and the perfect copy of his nature. . . ." (Heb 1:3).

Sanctifying Holy Spirit

IT IS we who have to become "perfect" as our Heavenly Father is perfect, to become "holy" as he is holy. Yet, as we saw in the life of Christ, we do not bring "our" holiness to God. Holiness, as Jesus experienced, is what God does to him and to us through his anointing Holy Spirit. The Holy Spirit anointed Jesus in his humanity and gave him the power to be holy as the Father is holy, in each moment of his earthly existence. The same Holy Spirit brings us his sanctifying power, making it possible with our cooperation to truly become holy as Jesus is holy.

This is seen especially when we are presented with "crosses," or sufferings, that seemingly go against our carnal-mindedness. But just as we learn in the Spirit of the risen Jesus to suffer with him in order to enter into his glory (Rm 8:17), so we will be empowered by the same Spirit to do works of holiness in such sufferings. The power comes to us through the Spirit of Jesus who suffered in order that in his glory he might give us his sanctifying Spirit. ". . . And so Jesus too suffered outside the gate to sanctify the people with his own blood. Let us go to him, then, outside the camp and share his degradation. . . . Keep doing good works and sharing your resources, for these are sacrifices that please God" (Heb 13:12-16).

The Spirit of the risen Lord brings us into the holiness of Jesus and that of the Trinity. Dwelling within us in deepest intimacy of total self-emptying love. God becomes present to us in his Spirit of love. He becomes present to us as holiness in his Spirit of love. Love bring communion and in this intimate union with the indwelling Trinity we can be made holy or sanctified to become "truly children of God" (1 Jn 3:1).

Summary

LET US SUMMARIZE the essence of God's holiness as we have tried, in this chapter, to develop this essential characteristic of God as a triune community of love. We have highlighted that God's holiness first stresses his awesome transcendence in his relationships with us, his creatures. God is one and many, a community of love made up of intimate personal relationships of Father, Son and Holy Spirit within the one Trinity. Creation is God extending such intimacy to his created human beings through the same self-emptying actions of Father, Son and Holy Spirit, operating as uncreated energies of love in the created world.

God As Wholly Other

GOD IS "wholly other," the Source of all being. We cannot possess God. He can only come to us as free, giving of himself in humble, self-sacrificing love. God's holiness, as revealed in the Old Testament, but, above all, through Jesus Christ's revelation in the New Testament, is the Trinity condescending to us, in our creatureliness and brokenness, in order to allow us to share his very own life.

Part of God's transcendent nature is seen in his very nature as love poured out in self-sacrificing on our behalf. His righteousness, or authenticity, as humble Gift to us in order that we might be able to enjoy eternal happiness by participating in his very nature (2 P 1:4), must abhor and resist any movement outside himself that is self-centered. Thus, God's holiness seeks to chasten us in our sinful pride.

His Spirit of love moves us, therefore, to a sense of sin and of our own inability to heal ourselves or "save" ourselves from such bondage. Abbot Pimen of the Egyptian desert put it succinctly when in the fourth century he declared what Scripture so often insists upon: "Weep for your sins. There is no other way to salvation." This *compunction*, or abiding sorrow for the godless past and the fear of a future without God against whom in his holiness we arrogantly have turned, allows us to contact God in our broken humility.

God gives himself to the weak, the poor, the needy, in a word, to the humble, because they have begun to enter into truth about God's great and perfect out-poured love for themselves and truth about their sinfulness. Crying incessantly with the penitent David, "Wash me clean of my guilt, purify me from my sin" (Ps 51:2), will gain us through the Holy Spirit a "second baptism" with its complete cleansing from all guilt and sin. Freed from such guilt, we are filled with great tenderness and longing for greater union with God. In our weakness, we truly find our strength in God's holiness.

Indwelling Presence

THE FINAL, main element in God's holiness is the experience through the sanctifying Holy Spirit that the Trinity dwells within his children, who have become holy by living as members in the Body of Christ, the only begotten Son of God. We Christians, in Jesus Christ, have the Way, the Truth and the Life that makes God's holiness, as most intimate self-giving presence, possible. Jesus, by his death and resurrection and the outpouring of his Holy Spirit, allows us to enter into the Holy of Holies, into the very heart of the indwelling Trinity, living at the center of our human consciousness.

The *Letter to the Hebrews* expressess the role of Jesus as the image of the Father and the access whereby we can enter into true holiness by dwelling in God's holiness:

> In other words, brothers, through the blood of Jesus we have the right to enter the sanctuary, by a new way which he has opened for us, a living opening through the curtain, that is to say, his body. And we have the supreme high priest over all the house of God. So, as we go in, let us be sincere in heart and filled with faith, our minds sprinkled and free from any trace of bad conscience and our bodies washed

with pure water. Let us keep firm in the hope we profess, because the one who made the promise is faithful. Let us be concerned for each other, to stir a response in love and good works (Heb 10:19-25).

Living In The Holy Of Holies

OVERWHELMED by God's holiness, we do not strive to be holy by doing "holy" deeds or works of holiness, as though God needs our sacrifice. We eagerly wish to obey the Divine Word, enfleshed for love of us to image God's holiness, as he directs us from within us through his Holy Spirit.

The place to which we go to enter into God's holiness is in our heart. By Jesus' indwelling oneness with us, by his death-resurrection and the gift of his Spirit, we now have the right to approach with boldness "into the sanctuary" by the blood of Jesus, our high priest.

We now have the power to become holy as God is holy. It is not by the power of our works that we become holy. It is in him, our powerful high priest, who intercedes for us, that the Father will release his Spirit, who will reveal to us that we now live intimately in God's holiness, One with Christ, we are one with the Trinity, Father, Son and Holy Spirit. We can now do all as a symbol of the return of ourselves totally to God as gift. We are possessed totally by God. We burn with passion still more to live only in Christ and no longer for ourselves (Gal 2:20).

We have been saved by Jesus' outpoured gift of himself on the cross. "He sacrificed himself for us in order to set us free from all wickedness to purify a people so that it could be his very own and would have no ambition except to do good" (Ti 2:14). Our salvation has been perfectly completed by Jesus Christ. God can do no more for us since his holiness has reached the peak of human expression in Jesus in outpoured love, freely given, that we might share his love.

As St. Paul writes, salvation is a gift from God in him, "not by anything of your own" (Ep 2:8). Paul specifies this in greater detail:

> But when the kindness and love of God our savior for mankind were revealed, it was not because he was concerned with any righteous actions we might have done ourselves; it was for no reason except his own compassion that he saved us, by means of the cleansing water of rebirth and by renewing us with the Holy Spirit which he has so generously poured over us through Jesus Christ our savior. He did this so that we should be justified by his grace, to become heirs looking forward to inheriting eternal life. This is doctrine that you can rely on (Ti 3:4-8).

Humbled by God's holiness revealed in Jesus Christ, we joyfully seek to respond to our being transformed into holiness as we seek to live lives of Christ-like holiness. We are God's work of art, created in Christ Jesus to live the good life as from the beginning he had meant us to live it" (Ep 2:10).

Now we can more easily, and in greater depth, understand how God's holiness makes it possible for God to be merciful towards us. Holiness and mercy with God, and in our own relationships with others, can never be separated.

CHAPTER THREE

Merciful God

You and I, as children, surely enjoyed reading fairy tales, those stories of archetypes that we meet so often emerging from our unconscious, especially in our dreams. I find, still as an adult, much pleasure and actual enrichment for my spiritual journey in rereading Grimm's Fairy Tales.

The Frog King is one of my favorites. In some versions, it is a beautiful princess who kisses a frog, a prince, upon whom a witch cast a spell and turned him into a frog, and he becomes a prince again. In Grimm's "original" tale, I discover a powerful insight I so readily apply to Jesus Christ.

Grimm's tale is about a most beautiful daughter of a king, ". . . The youngest was so beautiful that the sun itself, which has seen so much, was astonished whenever it shone in her face." While playing in the forest with her golden ball, it fell into a very deep well. She wept at her loss until a frog promised to fetch it, but only if she promised to love him and make him her companion.

When she obtained her ball, she ran away and tried to forget both the frog and her promise. The frog appeared while the family, with the King, were at table eating. The frog repelled her with disgust as he demanded to be her companion. Her good father, the King, insisted she fulfill her promises to the frog. When the frog wanted to sleep next to her in her own bed, she angrily threw the frog with all her might against the wall. Immediately, he turned back into a kind prince with beautiful eyes. She married him and lived happily ever after in his kingdom.

In prayer, I see how the Son of God, Jesus Christ, has become, not only human "by taking the nature of a slave...," but he also "humbled himself and became obedient to death; yes, to death on a cross" (Ph 2:7-9). It is our sins that brought the terrifying violent sufferings to the suffering servant of Yahweh: ". . . So disfigured did he look that he seemed no longer human" (Is 52:14).

> 'Who could believe what we have heard,
> and to whom has the power of Yahweh been revealed?
> Like a sapling he grew up in front of us,
> like a root in arid ground.
> Without beauty, without majesty (we saw him),
> no looks to attract our eyes;
> a thing despised and rejected by men,
> a man of sorrows and familiar with suffering,
> a man to make people screen their faces;
> he was despised and we took no account of him (Is 53:1-3).

In spite of what our sins have caused him ("Ours were the sufferings he bore, ours the sorrows he carried. . . ."

[Is 53:4]), God the Father "exalted him and had given him the name above all names, so that at the name *Jesus*, everyone in heaven, on earth, and beneath the earth should bend the knee and should publicly acknowledge to the glory of God the Father that Jesus Christ is Lord" (Ph 2:1-11).

In Jesus crucified do we come to understand, by the power of God's Spirit, what God's mercy really is all about. We see how the God-Man, imaging the mercy of his Father, tenderly with great compassion, wishes to suffer with us, to take upon himself our sins and miseries, in order to raise us up to an intimacy so great that he could reveal to us the Good News: "Anyone who loves me will treasure my message, and my Father will love him, and we shall visit him and make our home with him" (Jn 14:23).

Grace: The Holiness And Mercy Of God

WE ARE SEARCHING for deeper insights always about the same topic of God as free, unconditional love. Now we come to the central feature of this book about God's mercy. What we must say first is that mercy is a greater clarification of what God as grace and holiness generally means. We can look at God rather abstractly, or in very general terms, as graceful love, without specifically introducing the notion of mercy.

Yet, the grace and mercy of God, as biblical revelation highlights for us, always go together. When we describe God in his merciful actions toward his human children, we are touching the essence of divine love. Grace is God as self-gifting love that is free and unconditional. God's holiness moves that gift of God into a free and constant act of a superior being, God, toward inferior beings to share his trinitarian community of love in a fellowship that makes us truly "participators of God's very own nature" (2 P 1:4).

Mercy specifies this unconditional, free love as self-gift to share God's very nature with us human creatures by highlighting God's turning toward us in our misery. It describes our human and absolute inability to free ourselves from our own prison-like confinement in weakness and distress. But, above all, God's love becomes relational to concrete, needy human persons as God's mercy contrasts God's eagerness to condescend into our miseries in perfect sympathy and co-suffering with us.

This is an *exodus*, or pass-over movement of mercy, from out of the triune community to enter into loving actions that are not merely co-suffering with us in our misery, but actions that seek in humble service to free us from such confining sufferings.

Thus, we can see more clearly what mercy adds to God's grace and holiness. Grace is God in absolute, transcendent "otherness," coming down into the limited world of creatures in free and unconditional love. The holiness of God assures us that all God's actions are aimed at God's free desire to establish us as sharers in his fellowship, in his very nature as a loving, self-sacrificing community.

The Merciful Heart Of God

Now we can see more clearly what mercy adds to God's grace and holiness. Mercy adds what is implied, but not specified, in God as grace and holiness. Mercy is the Trinity, exploding in love to create and share its life with us human beings. Yet it stresses the actual historical context in which God finds us, not only as miserable and incapable to answering God's great election to be his loving children, but so often as actually resisting God's gift of Self. Mercy adds "feeling" to an abstract, philosophical concept of God. Mercy leads us deeper into the very "heart," the very essence of God at his deepest personality as Father, Son and Holy Spirit.

We begin to see God as suffering with us in our sad frustrations. Darkness is the archetypal symbol that is used in Scripture to refer to God as he humbly condescends to become present in his communicating love to us human beings. "Shadow," for example, in Scripture, is an image to express the special protection of God over his people. Reference to darkness surrounding God is a biblical way to expressing God's stretching out in affectivity, in caring, to be lovingly concerned and self-involving in giving himself to us.

The late Abraham Heschel, one of America's leading Jewish theologians, in his work, *The Prophets*, uses the word *pathos* to describe God's "being in a personal and intimate relation to the world . . . a living care, a dynamic relation between God and the world . . . (God's) constant concern and involvement . . . an emotional engagement." God as mercy is not only "sympathetic" in his desire to share with us our sufferings. He is also vulnerable, humble, waiting, ready to suffer the insolence and indifference we tend to show toward his loving concerns for us.

A Suffering God

THAT GOD in his humility freely consents to suffer with us, and for us on our behalf, can never be accepted by logical demonstrations of the demands of justice, but sheerly by the gift of the Holy Spirit. Like bolts of lightning illuminating the night's darkness, so God's humble goodness shines brilliantly to uncover our inner creaturely weaknesses and crippling guilt and sins.

But his merciful light is also his burning desire to enter into our miseries and to take them upon himself in order that, by such emptying love, he can heal and restore us to his eternal embrace as Father to child, bridegroom to bride. God's active mercy unveils God's essence as divine grace and holiness, but as enfleshed in heartfelt encounter with our brokenness and God's effective, powerful activity to wipe away our miseries, that we might enter into a true and happy union with him.

Mercy In the Old Testament

LET US TURN to Scripture in order to understand more fully the riches of God's mercy toward us. Most English translations of the Bible use the one term, *mercy*, to translate very inadequately the mystery of God's love for us as mercy. Biblical scholars agree that there is no adequate understanding of God's mercy that does not deal also with the Hebrew concept of God's convenant love expressed in Hebrew by the word *hesed*. But the same scholars do not agree on the exact meaning of this rich word.

The Septuagint translation of the Old Testament into Greek renders *hesed* by the Greek word *eleos*. Roman Catholics and Eastern Orthodox are familiar with the repeated liturgical phrase: *Kyrie eleison*, "Lord, have mercy!" Latin translators used *misericordia* as an equivalent of God's mercy as *hesed*. We must keep in mind, however, that there can be no one word or one simple understanding of the richness of God's intimate relations with us human beings in our many needs that is generally described in the Old Testament as *hesed*.

Its meaning can be discovered only by other words with which it is associated. Since *hesed* aims to describe the intricacies of God's affective, active and condescending love for us, we can expect no philosophical meaning or perfect consistency in its use and applications. The emphasis in the use of *hesed* is God's persistence and devoted love. *Hesed* is the act of loving kindness on the part of God in choosing Israel. Through his promise to use his might and mercy to support his people, he freely enters into a covenant of love with his human children. This is strikingly brought out in the tender words that Yahweh addresses to his spouse, Israel:

> I will betroth you to myself forever, betroth you with integrity and justice, with tenderness and love; I will betroth you to myself with faithfulness, and you will come to know Yahweh (Ho 2:19-20).

God's Fidelity

HESED IS ASSOCIATED always with the Hebrew concept of *'emet*, which usually implies God's fidelity, steadfastness and loyalty so that God's *hesed* endures forever.

God freely, out of his generosity as superior to us inferior human beings, does what he is not obliged, out of justice or out of a contract, to do. When the Old Testament presents God as "remembering" his covenant, it also stresses his fidelity, that knows no end of commitment and resolve to carry through with his promises.

Yahweh creates the rainbow as a sign of his fidelity toward his covenant with his people. "When the bow is in the clouds I shall see it and call to mind the lasting covenant between God and every living creature of every kind that is found on the earth" (Gn 9:16).

God's fidelity would be shown as Yahweh is touched by the sufferings of his people. "I have also established my covenant with them, to give them the land of Canaan. I have also heard the groaning of the children of Israel, whom the Egyptians keep in bondage; and I have remembered my covenant" (Ex 6:4-5).

God has backed up his covenant with a mighty oath and he will not go against his word, his pledge of honor: "For Yahweh your God is a merciful God and will not desert or destroy you or forget the covenant he made on oath with your fathers" (Dt 4:31). Isaiah, with language of great tenderness, more than a mother could ever have for the babe feeding at her breast, describes the fidelity God pledges toward his people.

> For Zion was saying, 'Yahweh has abandoned me,
> the Lord has forgotten me.'
> Does a woman forget her baby at the breast,
> or fail to cherish the son of her womb?
> Yet even if these forget,
> I will never forget you (Is 49:14-15).

The Bowels Of God's Mercies

A MOST INTERESTING Hebrew word is often used in the Old Testament to express God's mercy or pity toward his people, but with connotations of a tender, totally committed love as that of a mother for her child. This word is *rahamim*, the plural of the singular noun, *rehem*, which means womb or belly. For the Hebrews, the seat of deepest affections were the bowels or the entrails. This term of *rahamim* is used to describe that Yahweh loves his people more tenderly than a mother loves her child, a shepherd his sheep, a bridegroom his bride. He is desirous of doing all to remove pain and suffering from his children's lives and replace them with exuberant, rich, happy health. This tender love that is everlasting and so full of feeling in the heart of God toward his people is expressed by the prophet Jeremiah: "I have loved you with an everlasting love, so I am constant in my affection for you" (Jr 31:3). Again, the same prophet has Yahweh speak these words so full of feeling toward his children:

> Is Ephraim, then, so dear a son to me,
> a child so favored,
> that after each threat of mine
> I must still remember him,
> still be deeply moved for him,
> and let my tenderness yearn over him? (Jr 31:20).

A Covenant People

THE BEAUTIFUL CONCEPT of God's mercy, as we have said, cannot be seen, except through understanding of the *hesed* relationship of God with his people, and this especially in Yahweh's establishing a covenant with them. In *Genesis*, we see an ideal communion, pictured before sin had entered to disturb this loving union. God communicated himself to his children through his Word. He would progressively give himself to man and woman as he gives himself to his own Word within the Trinity. God walks with man and woman and dialogues with them in the cool of the day, a picture of peace and repose (Gn 2:8, 15). But before that familiarity could flower into a community of shared life through human obedience in fulfilling God's will in all things, sin entered into the hearts of the first man and woman.

Sin is an act whereby human beings close the spiritual ears of conscience to God's Word and seek to live their lives independently of God. They do not wish any longer to be present to God's loving presence. Although we human beings can never stop God from being present in his gift of himself to us as grace and holiness through his Word, it is we who can run from his presence as self-emptying gift and hide from his presence (Gn 3:10).

Through sin, we human beings begin our long pilgrimage in exile, absent to the God who is ever present to us. God continually speaks his Word; but we are deaf. God is present, touching us in millions of ways; yet we are blinded to His presence. God is still, however, a consuming fire (Heb 12:29) and burns ardently to be present as a gift of love to every human creature. He keeps the door open by promising the human race that he will establish a covenant. Through the offspring of the "woman," he would crush the head of the serpent (Gn 3:15). Sin would be vanquished and human beings would gain ultimate victory in being restored to God's living and loving presence.

The Hesed Covenant

GOD'S WILL TO SAVE, pardon and restore his children, according to his own image and likeness, becomes manifested in God's free election of his people that centers chiefly around his initiating and maintaining his covenant with constant fidelity and deep affection.

To understand *hesed* as a covenant of love, freely initiated by God in forgiving love toward sinful mankind, it would be helpful to realize the importance the idea of *covenant* played in Jewish history. In the early history of the Hebrews, their society had few, if any, written documents. The spoken word was ritualized to express an agreement that was more binding than a contract based on justice.

Through its ritual, there was usually a pouring out of the blood of some animals as a solemn sign of both parties pledging deepest affection and loyalty to each other, as though they were bonded almost as blood members of the same family through the outpoured blood.

We see in the Old Testament that the re-establishment of love between God and human beings was expressed through various covenants established freely by God's own initiative. God makes a covenant with Noah and, after the flood, he promises never again to strike down his living creatures (Gn 6:18; 8:21). As a sign of his covenant between Noah and his family, Yahweh makes the rainbow a sign to recall this covenant between himself and his creatures (Gn 9:16).

Covenant With Abraham

GOD CHOSE ONE MAN, Abraham, to be the father of his chosen people. In the story of God's covenant love with Abraham, we see the frequent pattern in the symbolized relations in re-established love between God and his people. There is first a calling, a free election on the part of God, who chooses Abraham and raises him to the dignity of father of God's unique people, a people who would be more numerous than the sands on the seashore and the stars in the heavens.

On the part of Abraham, there is a turning away from one style of life to a new life, a "conversion" toward God in total obedience to do whatever God would command. There would be duties and obligations to love God alone and to abandon all false gods. There was also an action that sealed the covenant between the two parties, God and Abraham with his posterity. And, finally, there was a commemorative sign, a lasting reminder of this bonding agreement, that would be the gift by God of the land of Canaan to his people and circumcision of all Jewish male offspring as a sign of the people's belonging to God's family.

This formula is seen in God's forming of his covenant with Abraham:

> I am El Shaddai. Bear yourself blameless in my presence, and I will make a covenant between myself and you and increase your numbers greatly. . . . Here now is my covenant with you: you shall become the father of a multitude of nations. You shall no longer be called Abram; your name shall be Abraham, for I make you father of a mutltitude of nations. I will make you most fruitful. I will make you into

nations, and your issue shall be kings. I will establish your covenant between myself and you, and your descendants after you, generation after generation a covenant in perpetuity to be your God and the God of your descendants after you. I will give to you and to your descendants after you the land you are living in, the whole land of Canaan, to own in perpetuity, and I will be your God. . . . You shall circumcise your foreskin, and this shall be the sign of the Covenant between myself and you (Gn 17:2-11).

Covenant With Israel

GOD RENEWED his lasting covenant with his people when he led them, through Moses, out of their slavery in Egypt and into the Sinai desert (Ex 19:1ff.). We begin to see two covenant rituals, expressed in *Exodus 24*. The more ancient ritual is the sprinkling of animal blood. Yahweh is represented by the altar upon which blood is sprinkled. Blood is sprinkled also upon God's people and they become, as it were, one blood, one family (Ex 24:3-8).

Another ritual symbol that evolved during the time of Moses and would be fulfilled so powerfully in the eucharistic banquet of the New Covenant is that of the ritualized banquet. In this symbol of covenant between God and his people, Moses, Aaron and his sons and the 70 elders, who represent the people and the priestly caste, share a meal in common with Yahweh (Ex 24:1-2, 9-11). In both these symbols, Yahweh pledges himself forever to be the God of his people. "You shall be my people and I will be your God" (Jr 7:23; 11:4; Ezk 11:20; 14:11; Ho 2:25).

The prophet Jeremiah introduces after the exile, a promise that God will not only re-establish his original covenant promises, but that God will confirm his covenant. He will do this no longer on tablets of stone. In the future, God will write his covenant in the hearts of flesh which his Spirit will give his people. "I will give them a heart to acknowledge that I am Yahweh. They shall be my people and I will be their God, for they will return to me with all their heart" (Jr 24:7).

Ezekiel prophesizes more specifically in anticipation of the New Covenant, through the release of the Holy Spirit, of God's future covenant within the hearts of the individual members of the Qahal, of the chosen people of Yahweh:

> I shall pour clear water over you and you will be cleansed; I shall cleanse you of all your defilement and all your idols. I shall give you a new heart, and put a new spirit in you; I shall remove the heart of stone from your bodies and give you a heart of flesh instead. I shall put my spirit in you, and make you keep my laws and sincerely respect my observances. You will live in the land which I gave your ancestors. You shall be my people and I will be your God (Ezk 36:25-29).

Jesus Is The New Covenant

How beautifully and powerfully God's mercy and love in his covenant with his chosen people progresses in a continued unveiling of his perfect, faithful, unconditional love until all his covenants would be fulfilled in the divine-human person, Jesus Christ. Jesus establishes by his free act of self-giving unto his own blood, the blood of God and man, the New Covenant between God and the human race.

We have seen how Abraham and Moses and the priests who followed the Mosaic covenant offered blood sacrifices of animals. Jesus gives his very own blood for the remission of sins and the life of the world. The writer of *Hebrews* shows us the uniqueness of the New Covenant in contrast with the Old:

> He brings a new covenant, as the mediator, only so that the people who were called to an eternal inheritance may actually receive what was promised. His death took place to cancel the sins that infringed the earlier covenant.... And he does not have to offer himself again and again, like the high priest going into the sanctuary year after year with the blood that is not his own. Instead of that, he has made his appearance once and for all, now at the end of the last age, to do away with sin by sacrificing himself. Since men only die once, and after that comes judgment, so Christ, too, offers himself only once to take the faults of many on himself, and when he appears a second time, it will not be to deal with sin, but to reward with salvation those who are waiting for him (Heb 9:15, 25-28).

This text shows the need in all covenants between God and his people, of death unto the outpouring of blood, for this is the ultimate human symbol of commitment and sincere fidelity: to live up to the promises given. But since Christ has died once, there is no more need for his continued death since Jesus has done "away with sin by sacrificing himself." St. Paul, in Galatians 3:15ff. and in Romans 11:6, shows how the sacrifice of Christ completes the Old Testament covenants and perfects them. The author of the

Hebrews holds that the Old Testament covenants are obsolete (Heb 8:13).

We could say that these two views do not contradict each other, but highlight one view over another as complementary. Redemption by the death of Jesus exceeds any other form, for it is no longer the levitical priesthood that offers the "alien" or non-human sacrifice, but Jesus Christ is the eternal high priest, since he is both God and man. Not only does he offer the sacrifice unto blood, but he, the high priest of all priests, offers and is the *victim* offered! The blood poured out over God's people is now the blood of God himself! Now we can most perfectly, through the Holy Spirit, who could not have been given until Jesus had died (Jn 7:39), see God as grace, as holiness, as mercy, and as righteousness, as we view Jesus on the cross.

The Good News is that now we have been redeemed by the mercy of God poured out in God's very own blood on our behalf. For this reason, God raised Jesus up in glory and gave him a name that is above every other name (Ph 2:9ff.). But now we have an eternal High Priest and there is no need of other high priests. "Then there used to be a great number of those other priests, because death put an end to each one of them; but this one, because he remains forever, can never lose his priesthood. It follows then, that his power to save is utterly certain, since he is living forever to intercede for all who come to God through him" (Heb 7:23-25).

God Is A Feeling God

JESUS IS the unveiling, the full revelation of God's love involving himself in our sufferings, miseries and sins to the point that he has personally taken

Merciful God 69

upon himself all our brokenness. Now, by his gift of himself, through his free death on the cross, we can be redeemed. In the New Testament, the general term, *mercy* of God, as revealed through the life, teachings and actions of Jesus on earth, is usually translated by the Greek words *eleos* and *oiktirmoi*. It is difficult to render an exact single translation into English that would do adequate justice to the richness implied in both these words. They both suggest a feeling and an action. The action flows out of this inner feeling.

We have already pointed out the word used in Hebrew in the Old Testament of *rahamim*, the plural of the singular noun, *rehem*, which means womb or belly. It highlights the intense affection of Yahweh that, according to Jewish belief, was situated in the bowels or entrails.

In the New Testament, the Greek writers used an equivalent translation in the word *splangchna*, which literally means, the bowels or entrails. This word is linked with the Greek words, *eleos* and *oiktirmoi* to stress the intense *feeling* and emotion God shows toward his suffering children and the emotions he shows as he wishes in mercy to suffer with them.

We see this word, *splangchna* used to express the immense compassion and sympathy that God, in the depth of his divine being, affectively has in his tender mercy and compassion for his human children. St. Luke uses this word to express the immensity of God's mercy. Fleist in his New Testament translation gives us this rendition: "Thanks be to the merciful heart of our God! A dawning Light from on high will visit us to shine upon those who sit in darkness and in the shadow and of death, and guide our feet into the path of peace" (Lk 1:78-79). Literally, the Greek original reads: "... You are to impart to his people knowledge of salvation through forgiveness of their sins, through the bowels (*splangchna*) of the mercy of our God...."

St. Paul also describes the intensity of God's actively concerned, suffering mercies when he writes to the Philippians: "For God is my witness. How I long for all of you in the *bowels* (*slangchnois*) of Jesus Christ" (Ph 1:8).

A Suffering God Of Mercy

I HAVE TAKEN SOME PAINS, without appearing too academic and pedantic, to highlight an element that was grasped by the writers of both the Old and New Testaments, but that I believe has been neglected in Western Christianity. That element of God's very nature as love is His immense, intense, tender loving mercy, which he wishes to show us, as he bends down to our miseries in order that he may take them unto himself, in order to relieve us of those miseries and bring us into true, eternal happiness in loving oneness with his triune community of love.

We find it very difficult to reconcile with God's immutable nature, as perfect and independent of all creatures, his will to be affected by us. God's will to be merciful is a will act, freely made by God to become concerned, affected, moved, changed, open to suffering and even rejection by us. It is a mystery that accepts God's essence as immutable; yet, in God's personalized uncreated energies of love, God as grace, God as community of love, stoops down in his mercy, not only to suffer with us in our distress, but also to wish with his power to alleviate us from our sins and miseries.

Jesus, Suffering Servant Of Yahweh

WE WILL NEED to devote a separate chapter on describing the mercy of Jesus as the image of God's mercy toward us. But it suffices, in this general introduction to the essential features of God's mercy, to summarize those elements by looking briefly at Jesus in his sufferings in order to see the unique element of mercy, so often lost to us of a more legalistic understanding of his infinite mercy toward us.

Can we not say that Jesus, becoming the suffering servant of Yahweh, freely wants to suffer and be poured out as spilt wax only because he wanted his human mind to be the perfect reflection of the Divine Mind? His human consciousness was to become one with the consciousness of the Father. Jesus in his merciful service to the world, entering into the very depths of sin and death and utter emptiness of self, was choosing humanly to be like God. It was the most perfect plan of imaging the eternal merciful love of the Father for you and me and all human beings. We have no other way of knowing the Father, but through the Son.

Here we have the perfect expression in human language of the very being of God as mercy. Jesus had said: "The Father loves me because I lay down my life in order to take it up again. No one takes it from me; I lay it down of my own free will. . . ." (Jn 10:17-18). The Father loves Jesus because he lays down his life freely in mercy, the tender compassion unto suffering that comes out of the very "bowels" of God's nature as divine. This love is so great which the Father has for us because Jesus makes concrete in human terms our Father's mercy toward us.

To Be Merciful Is To Suffer

IF THE FATHER loves Jesus because Jesus makes explicit the Father's moving mercy for us, is it too farfetched that the Father also undergoes suffering, seeing Jesus freely entering into the pit of darkness of human sinfulness and becoming a part of that for love of us? Can we not also accept the Father as a suffering servant on our behalf? Can we not suspect that, if God's very mercy for us pours out from the "bowels" of his being, from the depths of his divine nature, such mercy will call for, not merely pity, but real compassion unto personal suffering out of God's love for us?

It is true that the Father does not suffer physically since only Jesus is God-Man. But how can the Word serve by suffering for us human beings and the Mind that speaks that Word remain unmoved? Love cannot remain uninvolved in the sufferings of the one loved. The Father must be in his Word. He and his Son are one (Jn 17:22). The Word has meaning only because he is the exact Image of the Father, who communicates himslelf to us only in and through his Word.

Gerald Vann, O.P. Makes a good observation in discussing how God can sorrow with us:

> ... In the life of God there are no events; God has no history. Eternity is not an endless line running parallel with the line of time; it is a point; and what to us is past or future is as much present to eternity as is the actual moment we are now living.... Thus, the very immutability of God is not a denial of his involvement in the sorrows of these present times, but a triumphant vindication of it.

Of the human body of Christ you can say that first it suffered and then it was glorified and made glad; but throughout that temporal sequence the Godhead remains unchanged, and unchanged precisley in its knowledge and willing of, and its will to share in, that which Christ on the Cross took to himself and made his own and in his glorification turned into glory (Gerald Vann, O.P.: *The Pain of Christ and the Sorrow of God*; pp. 67-69).

For Me He Dies

THE FATHER is always speaking his Word. Jesus is always loving us with such tender mercy unto death. He is now present in our lives with that same dynamic, eternal love and mercy that he had when he died to serve us by his outpouring love unto death. In prayer, especially in the Eucharist, we can realize that we are *now* being loved by our infinitely, merciful loving Father unto the mad generosity of Jesus on the cross.

When we experience God's mercy unto death in order to take away our sins and bring us into true redemption and righteousness of true children of God, we can meaningfully say with St. Paul: "With Christ I am nailed to the cross. It is now no longer I who live, but Christ lives in me. The life that I now live in this body, I live by faith in the Son of God, who loved me and sacrificed himself" (Gal 2:20-21).

Such an experience leads me into the awesome presence of the Heavenly Father as perfect holiness, fullness of grace, beauty, love, in a word, active mercy. I realize that I am now being loved by my infinitely loving Heavenly Father through the service of the Suffering Servant of Yahweh, Jesus Christ.

A New Creation In Christ

SUCH a continued, experienced healing of our loneliness and self-absorption bursts the bonds that hold us imprisoned in our narcissistic prison. It begins a transformation of our lives which is a process shown by merciful service to others.

> . . . and the reason he died for all was so that living men should live no longer for themselves, but for him who died and was raised to life for them (2 Cor 5:15).

We can argue that the Heavenly Father will love us, if we are like Jesus in all things, especially in sharing somewhat in the mystery of his self-emptying mercy. We would be pleasing to the Father if we were like Jesus who is like the merciful Father. But I cannot be God's Word of self-emptying in order to serve, except in the context of serving my nearest neighbor.

As we experience this merciful love, like Jesus, we will want to live lives of self-emptying and living in mercy in service to the first person who enters our life. God is calling us to let his serving Word go among men and women, localizing his loving presence through you and me.

But before we look more specifically at Jesus and how he concretely lived to be God's mercy enfleshed in his concrete works of mercy on earth and also at our own works of mercy shown to others, we need to look at in the next chapter the last element necessary to understand God's mercy toward us. That element is God's righteousness which makes us righteous. We do not merely imitate Jesus, who imitates the merciful Father in condescending love by coming into our miseriess to share our brokenness. As God's active attempts to relieve us of such enslavement are accepted by us, we become transformed into merciful persons. We are called to become "righteous," redeemed, made whole, becoming truly a "new creation" in Christ (2 Cor 5:17) by God's gift of *righteousness*. We can be one with Jesus Christ, extending his very mercy into our broken world. We extend his mercy, yet we too, reconciled to God's great love for us through the merits of Jesus, can bring our gifted, righteous, new nature as our gift of mercy to others.

CHAPTER FOUR

God's Righteousness

In the Byzantine Liturgy of St. John Chrysostom, the deacon or priest invites the faithful at communion time to come forth to partake of the sacred banquet with these words: "Approach with faith and love and in the *fear* of God!" I often feel that, should there be any Western Christians participating in such a Liturgy, the phrase, "fear of God," would shock them. Why should a Christian have any fear of God at such a sacred moment as living members in the Body of Christ prepare to receive the gift of the risen Jesus, who gives himself to us as he did on the cross as outpoured love? Doesn't such perfect love cast out all fear, as John writes in 1 John 4:18?

The great early athletes of the Eastern deserts continually learned to cry out in tears and humility for Jesus, the Lord, the Christ, the Son of God, to show mercy upon them for their sinfulness. It isn't true that such mystics possessed a psychotic obsession with sin and an unhealthy sense of fear before a vengeful God. They understand, perhaps more than we do, that God's mercy is truly above all his works. They, however, could experience divine mercy only if they opened up in humility to cry out in a healthy fear that God's mercy and righteousness be harmonized in their lives.

From my studies of Eastern Christianity, I see a great need in our relationships with God and with neighbor to regard God's mercy as necessarily united to his righteousness. But do we really understand adequately what his righteousness means?

In the Western Church, we stress, in an almost exclusive way, God's beautiful mercy toward us. No matter how often or how greatly we have sinned against God, we believe he will always show us mercy and grant us his forgiveness. We call to mind the example of the prophet Hosea always forgiving over and over his adulterous wife, Gomer, as an image of God's everlasting, forgiving mercy toward us.

But do we really understand that God's mercy demands righteousness on his part? As God's grace precedes his holiness, so God's mercy precedes his righteousness, but neither can be separated from the other. Mercy and righteousness in Holy Scripture can never be conceived of without each other. As God truly is merciful toward us, so also he is righteous. He must conduct himself always, in showing mercy toward us that he is authentically divine and in harmony with his very nature as holy love.

God would not truly be merciful if he did not also hate sin, which goes against God's nature and our true nature, as God has created us to live in his perfect love.

Understanding The Concept Of Righteousness

TO UNDERSTAND righteousness and, therefore, to understand more fully God's mercy toward us, we must keep in mind the inner necessity of God's nature — as love, grace, holiness and mercy — to act always consistently with his being. God cannot show mercy toward us without his righteous nature demanding also a hatred of moral evil and a judgment with intent to punish and condemn what not only stands outside of his supreme will but, also, that which aggressively, in all absurdity, attacks his holiness.

We know from Scripture, and especially the preaching of the prophets of the Old Testament, that God does show mercy; but he is also a just judge. God judges the guilty, condemns the evil ways of sinners, and punishes those who violate his will. We will point out that this is not a primitive view expounded in the Old Testament, but replaced by the mercy Jesus came to teach us in the New Testament. On the contrary, we will see that Jesus becomes the focal point of God's fullest expression of both mercy and righteousness toward all human beings when the Son of God took our sins upon himself.

Righteousness In the Old Testament

LET US turn to study this theme of *righteousness* as found in Scripture, starting with the early understanding among the Hebrews in the Old Testament. By studying God's revelation, we will better understand the mercy of God, which cannot be shown to us, except in the context of God's righteousness.

When we read the Old Testament, we usually translate the very complex and rich notion of righteousness by the term *justice*. In Hebrew, the common word for righteousness is *sedek* and *sedakah*, or some cognates of these. The most fundamental idea has to do with meeting a standard, e.g., a weight is right or righteous if it is accurate, just, fair, correct, in a word, what it is supposed to be.

Yahweh "gives rain in righteousness" would mean, as in Joel 2:23, in his right, proper time and measure, out of his goodness to his people. When it is used in legal transactions, *sedek* is translated as just, or what touches on justice, as having a just or right claim (cf.: Dt 1:16; Lv 19:15; Pr 31:9; Ps 7:9; 18:21).

Job claims that he is innocent and righteous since he was not being punished by God for any offenses committed by him against God (Jb 9:2, 15, 20; 10:15; 27:6).

More specifically, righteousness found in a true Israelite is shown by proper conduct in obedience to fulfill God's law. To seek righteousness is to seek God's will as the true measure of one's proper nature as a member of God's chosen people. It is a sign of one's authenticity, both in God and in the chosen people, to live according to the measure of their true nature. We human beings are called to be righteous by obeying God as the ultimate Good in our lives.

When we are what we should be according to God's designs, God always will bless us abundantly. "For you, Lord, will bless the righteous; with favor you will protect him as with a shield" (Ps 5:13).

Righteousness in the Old Testament is often synonymous with salvation. Yahweh is our salvation; we are saved and granted security in God's salvific actions. "And the work of righteousness shall be peace, and the effect of righteousness, quietness and assurance forever" (Is 32:17; *KJV*).

God's Right Judgment

GRADUALLY, the righteousness of God is seen linked to his judgment passed on the "unrighteous," the sinners who disobey his laws. Such as virtue flowing out of God's very own nature balances out and gives firmness and "tough love" to God's mercy. In the Old and New Testaments, mercy can never become for the persons receiving it from God a self-centered comfort. It must flow out of God's "right" nature, out of God's condemning judgment and punishment of what goes against his holiness.

There can be no mercy without God's judgment, with himself as the measure of what is just and right. And this judgment contains a part of God's true, authentic love for his children. That is God's right, not only to discipline them, but to condemn and punish them out of his love for them. This is brought out in Solomon's prayer on the occasion of the consecration of the first Temple in Jerusalem:

> If any man trespass against his neighbor, and an oath be laid upon him to cause him to swear, and the oath come before your altar in this house: Then hear in heaven and do, and judge your servants, condemning the wicked, to bring his way upon his head; and justifying the righteous, to give him according to his righteousness (1 K 8:31-32).

We see in the Scriptures that this is a consistent part of God's condescending, merciful love. He despises, judges, condemns and punishes any kind of false idolatry or sinfulness in which an individual or the total community of Israel turns against God as the ultimate Source of all their being and happiness. Sin is a lie, insofar as it is not and never can be a part of God's economy of truth and grace. Sin is a rejection of the only real and lasting set of moral values. God, true to his being as love, grace, holiness and mercy, must abhor anything that is against himself in his intrinsic worth as the only, absolute Source of all life and true happiness for his creatures.

We see this righteous judgment of God on human sinfulness with God's active punishment when human beings commit sin and disobey him as told in the Genesis story. "Nevertheless, of the tree of knowledge of good and evil you are not to eat, for on the day you eat of it you shall most surely die" (Gn 2:17; Dt 27:26). Psalm 5 presents us with the consistent teaching in the Old Testament regarding the wrath and punishment that God inflicts upon those who turn away from obeying his will and of his blessings upon the righteous ones:

> You are not a God who is pleased with wickedness,
>   you have no room for the wicked;
> boasters collapse under your scrutiny.
>
> You hate all evil men,
> liars you destroy;
> murderers and frauds Yahweh detests.
>
> Yahweh, lead me in the path of your righteousness,
>   for there are men lying in wait for me;
> make your way plain before me.

> But joy for all who take shelter in you,
>   endless shouts of joy!
>   Since you protect them, they exult in you,
>   those who love your name.
>
> It is you who bless the virtuous man, Yahweh;
>   your favor is like a shield covering him
>   (Ps 5:4-6, 8, 11-12; Cf.: Ps 34-16).

Thus, we see that, both in God's mercy and his righteousness, God is true to himself as a loving, holy, graceful God, who shows severity in judging and punishing evil persons, while he blesses the humble, who worship him and cry out for his mercy and forgiveness. To them, God's righteousness will be given and they shall be righteous. God truly hears the cries of the poor!

Righteousness In The New Testament

As WE HAVE already pointed out, we must avoid any simplistic view that would present God's righteousness — as shown in the Old Testament — especially the idea of an austere, punishing God, as something exaggerated, not true to God's very nature, that Jesus' revelation replaces by a more merciful God, who passes no judgment nor inflicts any punishment on the sinful. This picture of God's righteousness in the Old Testament is consistent with one of the earliest of the New Testament writings: "It is certainly just for God to requite with affliction those that afflict you, and to reward with rest in our company you that are being afflicted. This will come to pass when the Lord Jesus is revealed in the sky amid flaming fire with his angels, heralds of his power. Then will he execute vengeance on those who know not God and submit not to the gospel of our Lord Jesus Christ. These will be punished with eternal ruin, far removed from the Lord's presence and the majesty of his might on that day when he comes to communicate his glory to all his saints and become the wonderment of all believers because of the faith you gave to the testimony we presented to you" (2 Th 1:6-10).

The New Testament consistently presents Jesus Christ, true God and true man, as God's righteousness incarnated. All the elements of the Old Testament concerning God's righteousness and mercy are retained, but receive a radical transformation because of God-become-flesh for us. In Jesus's teaching and actions of judging sinners during his earthly, public life, we see the same reality of God's righteousness as essentially a part of God's intrinsic worth. Jesus images the same nature of God as shown in the Old Testament. But now in the New Testament, we come to believe through Jesus' revelation that God is a triune community of love. God's righteousness comes to us from the Father through the Son in the Holy Spirit.

A Judging Jesus

MANY CHRISTIANS, reading the New Testament, are quick to select from the teachings and actions of Jesus those elements that appeal to them and bring them comfort. His own disciples were prone to do this in Jesus' own lifetime. We readily embrace those elements that present Jesus as merciful and all-forgiving of our sinfulness. He answers all our prayers.

But, we tend so readily to ignore the austere Jesus who still remains the living image of the Heavenly Father in his teachings on his judgment toward those who turn away from the ways of God. Jesus gives us the parable of the wedding feast to which a man came without a wedding garment, i.e., a person, who did not produce good works with faith, receives the terrifying condemnation: "Bind him hand and foot and throw him out into the dark, where there will be weeping and grinding of teeth" (Mt 22:1ff.).

To the dishonest servant who is unfaithful to the master's commands, the same sentence is given: to be cast out "where there will be weeping and grinding of teeth" (Mt 24:49-51). The foolish five virgins with no oil will receive from Christ the sentence: "I do not know you" (Mt 25:13). Those who did not perform kind works of mercy toward the least of Christ's brethren did not do it to him and receive a similar sentence: "And they will go away to eternal punishment, and the virtuous to eternal life" (Mt 25:46).

We see that both the Old and New Testaments give a consistent picture. God calls all of us his children to have faith, to focus all our attention upon God as the absolute Center in our lives, because God is love and is actively concerned for our happiness. This faith, also promises that God hears the cries of the poor and those, who in sincerity before God, seek his will. He delivers us from sin and punishment when we trust in him and live only for him and not for ourselves. Such faith also convinces us that God rightly and rightfully, as part of his merciful love, does judge, condemn and punish those who reject him.

A Sense Of Sin

IF KING DAVID could confess: "... I was born guilty, a sinner from the moment of conception" (Ps 51:5), so St. Paul could summarize the New Testament sense of sin in all human beings when he wrote: "... As through one man sin entered into the world and through sin death, ... Thus death has spread to all men because all have sinned...." (Rm 5:12).

Because we are tied to Adam's sin, all of us, according to Paul's teaching, find sin in our very members (Rm 7:24). There is that "unspiritual" self within all of us that Paul found dictating to him what he should do against God's law. He finds himself doing what he knows he should not do and not doing what he knows he should do (Rm 7:14ff.).

The sense of sin found in New Testament writings presupposes what is found in the Old Testament, but it adds a revolutionary concept to it.

In the Old Testament, there is no single word to denote *sin*. J. Pederson, in his work, *Israel I-II*, presents sin generally as a breach in God's loving and merciful covenant which he has made with his chosen people. The Hebrew words, *het'* and *hatta't*, which are translated in the New Testament by the Greek word, *hamartia*, means "to miss the mark." This removes the merely legalistic view of sin based on deliberation to commit sin and broadens it to embrace the cause of sin as anything that prevents a human being, or the people of God, from living with God as the Center. It is failure to attain one's goal, one's end. Thus, sin is unreality, insofar as it is considered "non-action" in regard to the "real" action that brings fulfillment to the individual person or the community.

An important Hebrew word for sin in the Old Testament that would provide a context for understanding the richness of the concept of sin in the New Testament is the word, *'awon*. This word connotes a deviation, an element of failure and of distortion of something that should never have come into existence.

Sin in the New Testament can refer to sin as a single act, sin as a state or condition, or sin as a power. These latter two ideas are found often in the Pauline and Johannine writings. But the radical newness presented by the New Testament writers, and not found in the Old Testament, is that God has sent his own Son to conquer and destroy sin in the lives of those who believe in him as the Son of God. The magnitude of sin and the slavery that keeps the human race in absolute bondage through sin are highlighted only to accept the power of Jesus Christ as God's righteousness for us. God through his Holy Spirit given us through Jesus' resurrection, redeems us and makes us righteous.

In the Old Testament, we see that only God can deliver us from sin. In the New Testament, the Good News is that God has done this through his Son, Jesus Christ. God, in his love, can do no more than He has already done for his people, his children, in giving them his Son as *Deliverer* and God's *Righteousness*.

St. Paul's Teaching On Righteousness

PAUL USES Old Testament terminology, but gives a revolutionary radicalness to the topic of sin and redemption because of Jesus Christ. We find stressed the same absolute impotence on our part to be "saved" by our good works, especially by observance of the Law.

In his letters to the Galatians and to the Romans, Paul clearly shows that it is not by observance of the Law, nor by our good works, that we are justified (cf.: Rm 3:11, 28; Gal 2:21, 16; 3:11).

But, part of the Good News is that a new and a perfect righteousness is brought to us by Jesus Christ. It is by faith in him, the Son of God, who dies to redeem us from sin, that we come to salvation. Paul quotes Habakkuk: "... The upright man will live by his faithfulness" (Hab 2:4; Rm 1:17). But he also insists that full faith be placed in Jesus Christ: "... Through our Lord Jesus Christ, by faith we are judged righteous and at peace with God, since it is by faith through Jesus that we have entered this state of grace in which we can boast looking forward to God's glory" (Rm 5:1-3).

Paul shows clearly that this new holiness and righteousness given to us through Christ Jesus is derived solely through our faith in him.

> For his sake I have suffered the loss of all things, and I count them as rubbish that I may gain Christ, and be found united to him, not with a holiness of my own derived from the Law, but with that which is obtained by faith in Christ, the holiness which God imparts on condition of faith (Ph 3:9-10).

This, by which we are made righteous before God and worthy of eternal life, is declared, also, by St. John to be surely God's gift to us in his Son and that, through our faith in him Who died for us, we gain such eternal life. "So marked, indeed, has been God's love for the world that he gave his only-begotten Son: Everyone who believes in him is not to perish, but to have eternal life. The fact is, God did not send the Son into the world to condemn the world. Not at all; the world is to be saved through him. He who believes in him is not liable to condemnation, whereas he who refuses to believe is already condemned, simply because he has refused to believe in the name of the only-begotten Son of God" (Jn 3:16-19).

Through Jesus, we receive God's very own life, through the baptism of his Holy Spirit, whereby we are reborn "from above" (Jn 3:3, 5). Jesus is God's righteousness made enfleshed (Rm 8:10). This new life of righteousness is God's gift to us through his Son. "The Son of God made his appearance for the purpose of destroying sin, the work of the devil. No one who is a child of God sins, because the life-germ implanted by God abides in him, and so, he cannot sin. He is a child of God.... Whoever fails to lead a holy life is no child of God, neither is he who fails to love his brother" (1 Jn 3:8-10).

Jesus Takes Away Our Sins

WHAT DOES IT MEAN in the Johannine and Pauline writings that Jesus has taken away our sins? In becoming human, he came under the Law. Taking on our human nature and born as we, Jesus Christ, the Son of God made man, has also associated himself with and has taken upon himself our "flesh of sin." The law of the spiritually-minded, which directs my life in Christ Jesus, has delivered me from the Law, which entices me to sin, and leads to death. What was impossible to the Law, in that it was helpless because of corrupt nature, God has effected. By sending his Son in a nature like that of sinful man and in order to remove sin, he has condemned sin by the incarnation, in order that the requirements of the Law might be fulfilled in us who live no longer according to our lower, but according to our higher nature (Rm 8:2-4). In our human nature before the incarnation, there was no power to be justified before God (Rm 3:20). There was only the power of sin in the body of flesh (Col 1:22).

Yet, God's great love and holiness in his burning desire to have mercy upon us gave us his Son to make us righteous before God by living, no longer we ourselves, but letting Christ live in us as we become co-crucified with him (Gal 2:19-20). He who is Judge is judged on our sinful behalf (Rm 5:6, 8: 8:3). He, the Just One and the Righteous One in whom there is no sin, stands in our sinful and unrighteous place (1 P 2:24; 3:18; Rm 6:10).

By his blood he justified us (Rm 5:9). The blood for Paul and for us should always symbolize the sufferings and death of Jesus on our behalf. In giving us Jesus as our propitiation-victim, God shows us how great is his love for us and his desire to share his very own life forever unto our perfect happiness. We must not picture the Heavenly Father as a tyrant who is delighted that the last drop of blood has been sacrificed on our behalf and is content that justice has been done.

As we contemplate prayerfully Christ's sufferings and death, freely taken upon himself for our sakes, we see the perfect love imaged by him of the eternal Father for us. This is what it costs God to be righteous and true to his nature. He wishes to destroy sin by his Son incarnating all sinfulness of humanity. The Father shows his righteous disdain for self-centeredness, the root of all sin. We begin to understand only in Christ, suffering on the cross unto his death, what sin is and how God by his very nature must resist it. Only in Jesus can we see God's full judgment on sin. Only in him can sin be taken away by the blood of the Lamb of God (Jn 1:29).

A Crucified God

JESUS had said to his disciples: "He who sees me sees the Father" (Jn 14:9). Our faith in Jesus, that he is truly one with the Father, of the same nature as the Father and his Spirit of love, allows us to see God's great love in the sufferings and death of Jesus. This is the amazing wonder of God's plan and the only way for him to accomplish his full grace, holiness, mercy and righteousness through his incarnate Word. Theologians dispute the possibility of other ways. Concretely, this is his way, chosen from all eternity to make us a "holy and spotless people" (Ep 1:4).

Only in Christ do we maintain God's faithfulness and our unfaithfulness. We see clearly the fullness of God's mercy which can never go against God's inner worth and dignity as his mercy shines through his righteous hatred for sin. Because Jesus Christ, God-man, is the Son of the Father, anointed in human form to express God's infinite love for his children, he is God's representative who guarantees God's love and mercy toward us. God truly dies for us!

Yet, Jesus is also one with us and is our representative. Moreover, he guarantees that God's righteousness is fulfilled as he dies for our sins. We can never doubt how greatly God despises and punishes sin. He assures us with absolute guarantee that, not by any of our acts, but solely through our belief in his act of accepting to be the universal sin of all human sinfulness, we are set free of our guilt and sins. We need fear God's judgment no more. We need only fear that we do not believe in his righteousness which Jesus won for us. And we show openly to God and the world around us whether we are righteous and living in God's righteousness by living in the power of the Holy Spirit to produce the fruit of the Spirit (Gal 5:22), and no longer living in guilt and sin.

The ancient prophecies, especially of the messianic Psalm 22 and those of Isaiah depicting the Suffering Servant of Yahweh, bring us new understanding of the atonement of Jesus on the cross, and how we are saved by "his blood."

> Without beauty, without majesty (we saw him),
> no looks to attract our eyes;
> a thing despised and rejected by men,
> a man of sorrows and familiar with suffering....
> And yet ours were the sufferings he bore,
> ours the sorrows he carried.
> But we, we thought of him as someone punished,
> struck by God, and brought low.
> Yet he was pierced through for our faults,
> crushed for our sins.
> On him lies a punishment that brings us peace,
> and through his wounds we are healed (Is 53:2-5).

For Me He Died

JURGEN MOLTMANN, in his classic, *The Crucified God*, presents a realistic picture of Jesus' terrifying sufferings, but placed properly in his relationships with the Father and us sinners. He writes: "His death was not a 'fine' death. The Synoptic gospels agree that he was 'distressed greatly and toubled' (Mk 14:33), and that his soul was sorrowful even to death. He died 'with loud cries and tears,' according to the *Epistle to the Hebrews*, 5:7. According to Mark 15:37, He died with a loud, incoherent cry. ... Jesus clearly died with every expression of the most profound horror. How can this be explained? ... We can understand it only if we see his death, not against his relation to the Jews and the Romans, to the law and to political power, but in relation to his God and Father, whose closeness and whose grace he himself had proclaimed. Here we come upon the theological dimension of his life and death. Mark 15:34 reproduces the cry of the dying Jesus in the words of Psalm 22:2: 'My God, why hast thou forsaken me?' This is certainly an interpretation of the Church after Easter and, indeed, Psalm 22 as a whole had a formative influence on Christian passion narratives. But it seems to be as near as possbile to the historical reality of the death of Jesus" (pg. 146-147).

The horrendous folly of the sufferings and death of Jesus on the cross is sheer wasted pain except in terms of the logic of love! We now have the way whereby we can be redeemed and set free of our slavery to sin and selfishness. Jesus' *kenosis* (Ph 2:8), or self-emptying, even to the last drop of blood and water, brings us through the illumination of his Spirit to a realization of the free love of God in his mercy toward us in our bondage to sin, as he takes upon himself, in Jesus, all our sins. In Jesus, all sins have been taken away before the righteous Father. We have them forgiven subjectively only as we cry out in our fear that we might turn back toward selfishness and that Jesus come and be our strength. We "believe in him" by accepting in the moments of trials and temptations the Trinity's manifested loving mercy and righteousness in Christ Jesus.

In view of such constant love of the indwelling Trinity, we can progressively be healed of our sinfulness, as we seek in the "new creation" that we are in Jesus Christ (2 Cor 5:17) to live genuinely as God's children. The mercy of the triune God has been perfectly and completely manifested in Jesus' death. By his resurrection and outpouring of his Spirit, we can live in this reconciliation with the indwelling Trinity. Sin will no longer have a hold over us for Jesus' Spirit reveals in each moment, in each human situation, how beautiful we are in Christ Jesus. We experience God's distaste and condemnation of sin and we, too, hate all sins.

As living members of his body, we live by our true uniqeness in Jesus, as we obey his commandments to bring forth works of love that flow out of our new, regenerated nature. Freed by Christ from slavery to sin, we Christians become slaves to righteousness and to God, as Paul writes in Romans 6:15-23. We live in the continued experience that we really are children of God, even now (1 Jn 3:1).

We live out the words of St. John: "No one who is a child of God sins, because the life-germ implanted by God abides in him, and so, he cannot sin. He is a child of God. Here is the sign which reveals who are God's children and who are the devil's: 'Whoever fails to lead a holy life is no child of God, neither is he who fails to love his brother' " (1 Jn 3:9-10).

This proof, as we will show in another chapter on our response to God's mercy and our acceptance of his righteousness, and whether we truly are righteous through Christ's Spirit, will be measured by our corporal and spiritual works of mercy that flow from our proper nature. If we are transformed by Christ and live in him through his Spirit, one with our Heavenly Father, we must be authentic and true to ourselves, who are being created always by, and in, and through God's Word, Jesus Christ.

If God's mercy and righteousness are believed in by us, we must be true to our nature that shows mercy and righteousness in every thought, word and deed in our relationships towards others. A fitting conclusion and summary of this chapter on God's righteousness is from the First Epistle of John:

> We know what love is from the fact that Jesus Christ laid down his life for us. We, too, ought to lay down our lives for our brothers. . . . Little children, let us not love merely in word or with the tongue, but in action, in reality. . . . His commandment is this, that we should believe in the name of his Son, Jesus Christ, and love one another, as he commanded us. He who keeps his commandments abides in God and God in him. It is the Spirit abiding in us who gives us the assurance that God abides in us (1 Jn 3:16-24).

CHAPTER FIVE

God's Merciful Forgiveness

Reflecting over the past years of my life, I have finally begun to see a consistent principle at work in my relationships toward God and my neighbor. I smilingly refer to this as "the Maloney Law," because I have discovered it operating in *my* life with the irrevocable consistency of a law, therefore, it is *my* law, working uniquely within me. But you, dear reader, can substitute your name for mine and know it is also *your* law!

It goes like this: As we relate to God, so we relate to our neighbor. As we experience God, as an object, extrinsic to us, from whom we seek to receive pleasant and good things, that is also predominantly how we experience others around us. As we experience God's forgiving love for us, we will be transformed by his love to be able consistently to show forgiving love toward other human beings.

The Meaning Of God's Forgiveness

BUT what does it really mean that God forgives us? We have already seen that God is love by his very nature or his proper *being*. Although his love manifests itself in any given moment of our historical lives, yet God is love (1 Jn 4:8) by his very being. He does not begin to love us, that is, to have a new and different attitude of self-giving of himself to us in this moment than from yesterday's moments.

As God is always eternally active, self-emptying love within the Trinity in interpersonal relations between the Father and the Son in the bonding love of the Holy Spirit, so the same trinitarian life of Father, Son and Holy Spirit is always being actively poured out in uncreated energies of love toward us. We are constantly inundated, invaded, bombarded by God's personalized love in each event of our daily lives. Thus, we do not have to ask God to love us, to give us "grace," show his face kindly upon us. We are always surrounded by God's being as self-giving grace, the gift of himself gratuitously given to us and not "earned" by anything we can do to merit his love. God cannot but be always loving us.

The mercy of God adds the dimension or specifies God's love as self-giving to us in our miseries and basic inability to help ourselves become our true selves in his trinitarian life. We cannot ask for this, since God's mercy is always present toward us in our many miseries and needs. When he comes to us out of his righteousness, his rejection of sin as opposed to his holy, loving nature, we call his mercy *forgiveness*.

Forgive Us Our Trespasses

WE FIND in the *Lord's Prayer* more than a mere prayer given to us by Jesus to be repeated rote-like. It is a beautiful compendium of the proper attitudes and relationships toward God our Father and toward our neighbors we should have, just as Jesus lived them in his earthly life. It is in this basic prayerful relationship toward God as forgiving Father that we find a difficulty. We pray that God will forgive us our trespasses as we forgive those who trespass against us.

Does this mean that God's forgiveness depends upon our acts of forgiveness toward others (cf.: Mt 6:9-13; Lk 11:2-4; Mk 11:25)? We must insist that, basic to Jesus' teaching in the New Testament, there is the necessity on our part to have an active compassionate concern for our brothers and sisters as God does. We must have a forgiving heart toward those who hurt us. This is not only the state of entering into eternal life, the eschatological community of brothers and sisters in our "elder brother," Jesus Christ. It is also the necessary condition for our being truly open and ready through repentance to turn away from our own self-centered sinfulness by being open to the constant love of God, always present and able to be experienced by us through his constant forgiveness and compassionate concern for us in our miseries.

Thus, we can say that to receive God's forgiveness is not an effect dependent upon our causality of forgiving first the "debts" of others who have injured us. The *Our Father* prayer is rather an example, or paradigm, of God's forgiveness which then should be ours through a continued state of repentance. This repentance is a gift from God's Spirit and we need to pray for it. But we, too, must commit ourselves to turn away from our sinfulness and turn toward God's forgiving love to be transformed into a forgiving love by God's loving, forgiving mercy.

St. Paul makes this clear when he writes: "Bear with one another and forgive whatever grievance you have against each other. Just as the Lord has forgiven you, so you must forgive" (Col 3:13). God, in Jesus Christ, is the model for our forgiveness. We cannot merit his forgiveness. We are to be transformed by God's loving and forgiving us first and always so we can exercise such forgiving love toward others.

God First Loves Us

ALL FORGIVENESS, like all love, originates in God, who loves and forgives us first. "Beloved, let us love one another, because love takes its origin from God. . . ." (1 Jn 4:7), (cf.: Lk 7:47; Mt 18:23-25). When we love and forgive our neighbors, God's love and forgiveness are made perfect in us (1 Jn 4:12). Our experience of God's loving forgiveness is intensified and our capacity to love and to forgive is increased.

If, however, we refuse to forgive others, we shall no longer experience the forgiveness of God, not that God refuses now to forgive us in love, but we ourselves have made it impossible to be open to receive what always is there, active and present, namely, God's forgiving love. The sun is always shining, but it is we who can hide away from its rays or close our eyes to its light.

To forgive our neighbor any injuries caused to us is our response to our experience of God's forgiveness which

God's Merciful Forgiveness

always precedes anything we do and is always present in its full gratuitousness. By being forgiven through a repentant spirit, we set up a movement within our hearts. Human forgiveness originates always in the intensity by which we experience, through God's Spirit, God's forgiveness. This feeds back into our experience, creating new possibilities of forgiveness.

Thus, New Testament teaching on forgiveness is not contradictory. The confusion arises from the fact that such teachings describe different moments in the cycle of forgiveness and different segments of the spiral. We must always insist that our forgiveness shown to others can never be the result of our efforts to earn God's love or out of fear of losing it. It is always the outcome of experiencing the free and gracious forgiveness of God.

Only the person who has experienced forgiveness from God or neighbor can truly forgive. It is the same as the principle that only one who has experienced true love can truly love (Lk 7:36-50). Experiencing God's forgiveness is a pre-condition for our forgiveness of others. But in our human experiences we meet God's forgiveness, more manifested and perfected, in our relationships with our fellow human beings. We love God by loving our neighbor (Mk 12:38). We experience God's forgiveness as we forgive others who have injured us (Mt 6:14-15). We seek reconciliation with God only when we have been reconciled with those whom we have injured (Mt 5:23-24).

Forgiving Others Means Not To Judge Them

THEREFORE, we see that forgiveness in the New Testament comprises both the readiness on our part to forgive those who have injured us and, also, to seek pardon of those whom we have injured. Both are necessary if the obstacles preventing us from experiencing God's constant forgiving love are to be removed. This is why a repentant and a broken heart is necessary to turn toward God and confess our sinfulness and utter inability, on our own strength, to be consistently loving without God's mercy.

We learn about and experience God's forgiveness when we begin to get in touch with our sinfulness and miseries. When we claim our sins before God and cry out for his healing forgiveness, we are in a position to accept God's forgiveness and that of others as well. We forgive others only when we have learned to forgive ourselves. We love others as we love ourselves. We hate others as we hate ourselves!

Thus, the Gospel gives us a constant teaching of Jesus that, in order to receive God's forgiveness and to forgive others, we must cultivate a non-judgmental attitude, first, toward ourselves and then toward others. Forgiveness is, in a word, non-judging. "Again, do not judge, and you will not be judged; do not condemn, and you will not be condemned; acquit, and you will be acquited. Give, and you will receive; a goodly measure — pressed down, shaken together, running over — will be poured into your lap. the measure you use in measuring will be used to measure out your share" (Lk 6:27-28).

How are we able to become non-judgmental toward others? The first and most important step is to realize we are as sinful as others. St. Paul teaches a universal sinfulness of mankind (Rm 5:12-21). St. John's *First Epistle* expresses the same truth in a slightly different manner:

> If we should say that we are not guilty of sin, we deceive ourselves, and the light of truth is not within us. If we openly confess our sins, God, true to his promises and just, forgives us our sins and cleanses us from every stain of iniquity. If we should say that we have never been guilty of sin, we make him a liar, and his message does not dwell within us (1 Jn 1:8-10).

We must not judge others because we simply cannot read their hearts (Mt 7:1). Only God knows the individual heart where alone the ethical quality of an act is determined (Mk 7:14-23). We forgive others by not being judgmental because we have no right to judge and no knowledge of all the factors that would possibly explain the words and deeds of others. How could we ever know the intricacies of God's graces given and an individual's cooperation or refusal to cooperate?

Therefore, at the heart of our forgiveness shown toward others, especially those who do evil to us, is always to assume a non-judgmental attitude in our thoughts. It is a silent observation of a fact which we cannot ignore, but we make no judgment on the inner motivation of the action or omission of a person. This must never mean that we approve of evil by a cowardly silence. Forgiveness in the New Testament never excuses nor tolerates sinfulness. It simply overcomes it with forgiving love. St. Paul gives us the principle to follow: "Be not conquered by evil, but conquer evil by good" (Rm 12:21).

Healing And Forgiveness

OVER and over in the Gospels, Jesus not only healed multitudes of people who came to him to seek healing but, Jesus, as part of his healing ministry, forgave them their sins. We could point out a few instances of this as representative of Christ's mission, stemming from his nature as both God and man. He heals the paralytic in Mark 2:1-12 and forgives his sins by making this forgiveness visible through a visible healing of the body. All of Jesus' healing were symbols of his forgiveness of sins which restored the sick to friendship with God.

In Luke 7:36-50, we read the narrative of the sinful woman who anointed Jesus' feet. Because she loved much, much was forgiven her, while Simon the Pharisee did not admit his sinfulness and he was not forgiven. Zacchaeus experienced the acceptance of forgiveness from Jesus and this radically changed his life (Lk 19:1-10).

The greatest healing power of Jesus passed on to generations of his sincere followers consisted in the social effects his forgiveness would have on society and, therefore, on the establishing of the future, eschatological community of love that he called the Kingdom of Heaven. In a world of violence that has only increased beyond all proportions in our times, Jesus broke the bondage and ignorance that covered all human beings by the law of the jungle, the *lex talionis*, which the Old Testament taught: an eye for an eye and a tooth for a tooth. He was the image of the unseen Heavenly Father who lives by non-violence toward all his children. He is unlimited love and mercy and, in Jesus, he manifested this by living unto the extreme of non-violence. Especially on the cross, Jesus pleads with his Father to forgive them for they do not know what they are doing in killing him or anyone else.

Jesus does not deny the offenses. He merely denies violent actions the power to dictate and dominate the lives of human beings. As he hung dying on the cross, Jesus began a way of life that would lead to true life. Mercy and forgiveness are the only ways to bring healing to society and inaugurate the Kingdom of Heaven. Our old self, however, seeks to live according to the dictates of the "false ego." I determine what is just and, therefore, I believe I can use violence to obtain what is my due.

Jesus shows us a new possibility that reveals the inner heart of God himself. This way, he guarantees his followers will transform their lives, as well as society, into true happiness. It is a call to take up the cross that is necessary in order that all men and women might live in merciful love toward each other, as he did. His Spirit would give his followers the power to accept the pain and the bitterness of offenses and to transform them into joyful suffering out of love for all human beings.

Be Converted And Become As A Little Child

CHRISTIAN mercy and forgiveness shown toward others is, in the teaching of Jesus, a duty within the Christian community. Chapter 18 of Matthew's Gospel gives us the characteristics of true Christian forgiveness. But, before Jesus gives a series of examples to illustrate true forgiveness, he demands a conversion: "I tell you frankly, if you do not change and become like little children, you will not enter the kingdom of heaven" (Mt 18:3). He calls us to a life of simplicity to live as children live. Jesus calls his followers to enter into a repentance through a continued process of conversion or turning away from our false pride and selfishness to begin to live as he did, in self-sacrificing love.

What does Jesus in his preaching and what do the teachings of the early Church mean by the term, *repentance*? From the Old Testament, repentance means, in general, a change of mind or heart, of intent, disposition, attitude, regret, a conversion and sorrow for sins. In the Old Testament, this concept is applied in a human way of speaking about God to God himself, who "repented" of his plan to punish persons or nations by destructive means. "Yahweh looked and thought better of this evil; and he said to the destroying angel, 'Enough! Now withdraw your hand' " (1 Ch 21:15; cf. also Gn 6:6; Jr 26:13; Ps 106:45).

In the Old Testament, we often see that repentance is accompanied by cultic liturgical practices that externalize what always should have been an internal conversion away from sin. Such practices were frequent fasting on account of the sins of an individual or a nation with all its people, cries and wails, beating one's breast, wearing ashes and sackcloth, often accompanied by public confession of one's sins.

In Hebrew, the word *sub* refers to a turning away from one's sinful self to put on a new, inner attitude. It refers to the letting go of previous attitudes and habits that came out of an "adulterous heart." God is very active in bringing about a conversion as we read in the passionate description of Yahweh's love and forgiveness toward his unfaithful wife, Israel.

> That is why I am going to lure her
> and lead her out into the wilderness
> and speak to her heart.
> I am going to give her back her vineyard. . . .

there she will respond to me
as she did when she was young,
as she did when she came out of the land of Egypt
(Hos 2:17, 15).

God would give his people a new heart (Ezk 36:26) and, also, a new heart to King David (Ps 51:12) as he cries out for forgiveness and forsakes sin.

Repentance Through Jesus Christ

WE SEE in the beginning of Jesus' preaching and that of John the Baptist, the constant call for the people to repent and believe in the Good News. "The time of waiting is over; the kingdom of God is close at hand. Change your evil ways; believe in the Good Message" (Mk 1:15; cf.: Mt 3:2-11; 4:17; Lk 3:1-14).

Jesus came to call, according to St. Luke whose Gospel is that of God's mercy and human repentance based on God's forgiving love, not the "righteous," namely, those who considered themselves sinless by observing the externals of the Law, but sinners (Lk 5:32; 5:8). There was an absolute necessity for repentance or else an individual would suffer eternal damnation or perdition (Lk 13:3-5).

The publican in the rear of the synagogue, ashamed of his sins, refuses to look up toward God on high, casts his eyes to the earth while he strikes his breast and confesses: "O God, have mercy on me, the sinner" (Lk 18:13). Jesus tells us that the pharisee, full of pride and self-centeredness, with no love for the sinner, the publican, in the rear of the synagogue, went away unforgiven, for essential in the mind of Jesus to repentance is a humble, poor spirit. "Everyone who exalts himself shall be humbled, and he who humbles himself, shall be exalted" (Lk 18:14).

Metanoia

THIS REPENTANCE that Jesus calls all of us to is expressed in Greek in the New Testament generally by the word, *metanoia*, or derivatives of it. It means a change of heart, a returning to a human being's true self, by a return with full awareness toward God. Although God is always releasing his Spirit of love to enlighten us as to our brokenness and incompleteness, we must begin by an honest look at our existential place in time, our being-in-the-world as "thrown" or unauthentic, as Heidegger describes the normal lot of human beings.

In Jesus, God's forgiving mercy came down and dwelt among us. He, the Way, the Truth and the Life (Jn 14:6), holds out to all of us down through all ages the possibility of accepting his call to leave the husks of swine, and rise, and come back to the Heavenly Father.

The first aspect of a true conversion, where we discover the Spirit of love operating within us, is to instill in us an anxiety, fear, disgust, as we confront our existence in any given time and place of our earthly existence in the light of our "non-being," our unauthentic self, not created by God. It is an ontological "nostalgia" to rise from slavery to selfishness and the pleasures of this world and return home to our Heavenly Father. Only in this way will we discover our true selves in our loving obedience to our Heavenly Father.

This first movement of true repentance is the soft dew of God's grace falling upon the hard desert floor of our hearts to stir the seeds planted there when we were made "according to the image and likeness" (Gn 1:26) of God. In repentance, there is always the Holy Spirit's gift of hope that we do not have to continue living such a low level of existence, riddled by fears and guilt, separated from all the persons whom we daily meet in a suspicion of threatening attack that makes us defensive and forces us to hide behind masks and walls which fill us with even greater fears.

Crying Out For A Savior

THE SECOND PHASE of true Christian repentance is to call out for the Savior, Jesus Christ, God and man, who alone can forgive all our sins and transform us by God's very own forgiving mercy into children of the loving, eternal Father. We are to show this new birth from above by showing forgiveness and mercy to all human beings. Once we have become completely convinced by the power of the Holy Spirit that we cannot save ourselves, the same Spirit convinces us that Jesus is the Source of our repentance. He takes away our sins and brings us new life, more abundantly.

Only when we realize that our false ego has been so powerfully in command and that we cannot extricate ourselves from such an interior imprisonment, then we will realize we are in need of a savior more powerful than we ourselves (1 Jn 4:4). He can bring us to our true self, which cannot exist outside of a loving communion with him in whom all things are reconciled to the Father.

Our great strength, as Mary Magdalene, the good thief on the cross, and St. Paul understood, is in our weakness.

Our strength is not to be found in our own power to remain in control, or in our own self-righteousness. God judges our readiness to accept his love and take risks to live in that love, rather than to place our justification in our perfect observance of some extrinsic law.

St. Paul well understood his own sinfulness and weakness, yet he placed all his strength in Christ:

> So I shall be very happy to make my weaknesses my special boast so that the power of Christ may stay over me, and that is why I am quite content with my weaknesses, and with insults, hardships, persecutions, and the agonies I go through for Christ's sake. For it is when I am weak that I am strong (2 Cor 12:9-10).

Toward A Lasting Conversion

BY CONVERTING our "unreal self" of sinfulness and self-centeredness into a burning desire to discover our true happiness in God's perfect love, we can enter into a new regeneration. St. Augustine expresses how the decision to surrender all, even our sinfulness, to God's love, is rooted in trust of God's unconditional love.

> I am so sure of thy love that I dare to come to thee even with my unfaithfulness; thou art able to love even my infidelity (*Enarrationes in Psalmos*).

We need, however, more than a mere desire to accept our brokenness and to believe that Jesus has "done it all." Our decision to put on our true self in Jesus Christ must be backed by a continual process of standing inwardly attentive to areas of falsity and courageously uprooting them from our hearts.

Union with Christ and life in him cannot come about, unless we embrace the conditions that he laid down if we are to possess our true selves in him. "If anyone wants to be a follower of mine, let him renounce himself and take up his cross and follow me. For anyone who wants to save his life will lose it; but anyone who loses his life for my sake and for the sake of the gospel, will save it (Mk 8:34. Cf.: Mt 10:38; 16:24; Lk 9:23; 14:27).

An Inner Light

As JESUS, in his humility, turned into the depths of his being and, in the Father's Spirit of love, heard himself as the Word, perfectly issuing forth in harmony and congruence with the mind of the Father, so we are to be attentive at all times to God's voice within us.

This indwelling presence of the glorious Christ is an inner light guiding us at all times. We can, in his Spirit, easily discern what is truly real from what is false and illusory, what is of his Spirit of love and what is of the spirit of darkness. Simone Weil (+1943), the Jewish mystic so drawn to Catholicism, wrote:

> We live in a world of unreality and dreams. To give up our imaginary position as the center, to renounce it, not only intellectually, but in the imaginative part of our soul, that means to awaken to what is real and eternal, to see the true light and hear the true silence. A transformation then takes

place at the very roots of our sensibility, in our immediate reception of sense impressions and psychological impressions. It is a transformation analogous to that which takes place in the dusk of evening on a road, where we suddenly discern as a tree what we had at first seen as a stooping man; or where we suddenly recognize as a rustling of leaves what we thought at first was whispering voices. We see the same colors, we share the same sounds, but not in the same way.

Christ's Atonement

ALL too often we have misunderstood God's forgiving love and the role of Jesus Christ in atoning for our sins. As we have pointed out, God's forgiveness is not a single act that God begins to do toward us when we have cried out for his forgiveness. As Mary, the Mother of Jesus, sang in her *Magnificat*, so we, too, when we are humble and poor in spirit, discover God's merciful and faithful forgiving love as constant and always present in God's active concern to bring us into fullness as sharers of his divine life.

> How sublime is what he has done for me,
> the Mighty One, whose name is 'Holy!'
> From age to age he visits those
> who worship him in reverence.
> His arm achieves the mastery:
> he routs the haughty and proud of heart;
> he puts down princes from their thrones,
> and exalts the lowly;
> he fills the hungry with blessings,
> and sends away the rich with empty hands.

He has taken by the hand his servant Israel,
and mercifully kept his faith
— as he had promised our fathers —
with Abraham and his posterity
forever and evermore (Lk 1:49-55).

When we humbly, by the work of the Holy Spirit, accept our sinfulness and our inability to heal ourselves of our false self, locked into a slavery of self-centeredness, the main obstacle preventing us from receiving God's forgiving mercy is overcome. It is true that Jesus Christ only once died on the cross for us. He in human form perfectly imaged the love of the Trinity for each of us as he reached his hour of total self-emptying love. Objectively, he has done it all for us! He has taken upon himself all our sins. He is the sacrifice to the Father that takes away our sins. God can do no more, nor is there need for Jesus ever to suffer and die again.

His sacrifice is perfect and finished. "It is now completed" (Jn 19:30), Jesus spoke to the Father and now he wishes the entire human race to hear the Good News on our behalf. Jesus has atoned, as high priest and victim, Giver and Gift, for our sinful pride. We can do nothing to merit God's forgiveness and mercy. God is love and mercy by being God. God's divine nature demands such love and mercy, not as an individual action that begins and stops, but as a part of God's very being, his nature as Beauty ever ancient!

Infusion Of The Holy Spirit

THIS GOOD NEWS is revealed to us in prayer by the Holy Spirit dwelling within us (Rm 8:9).

It is the Holy Spirit moving faster than the speed of light through our brokenness and non-reality, on wings infinitely bright, illuminating the core of our hearts. But it is up to us vigilantly to war against the strategy of the false ego that refuses any repentance and any surrendering on our part in child-like trust and obedience to the Heavenly Father.

As we stand guard to cut out of our lives any negative, unreal self-centeredness, we present ourselves in all our objective weaknesses and miseries before Jesus our Savior. It is the Spirit who pours into our hearts faith, hope and love to witness that Jesus is the manifestation of the Father's infinite, forgiving love for each of us.

In the Spirit, we can cry out, "*Abba* Father!" (Rm 8:15ff.), knowing we are truly children of God, heirs of Heaven and co-heirs with Christ forever.

Forgiveness Of Others

THE TEST of how Jesus' atonement for our sinfulness has been effective in our lives and how we have become transformed by God's love manifested to us in Christ Jesus, can be seen only in our daring to forgive those who injure us, those who "trespass against us." Loving one's enemy is the true index of how forgiving we are toward others and how much of God's infinite, forgiving mercy we have truly accepted through repentance into our lives.

> You have heard it said: 'Love your neighbor, and hate your enemy.' I, on the contrary, declare to you: love your enemies and pray for your persecutors, and thus prove yourselves children of your Father in heaven (Mt 5:43-45).

We go against our "worldly" logic to accept a lifestyle similar to that which Jesus lived. His style is the most perfect imaging of the Father's non-violent and forgiving mercy shown to us (Mt 5:39ff.). We are to show mercy and concrete forgiveness to those who reject and persecute us. We wish to enflesh the Heavenly Father's universal will that wishes all men and women to be saved (1 Tm 2:4).

Let us now turn to study the forgiving style of the life of Jesus lived as an imaging of the Father's mercy in human form. We open up to contemplate him as the image of God's mercy, which we are able to experience and transform by God's forgiving love through our continued repentant spirit. But, let us also thoroughly understand Jesus' clear teaching on merciful forgiveness in our daily relationships toward others.

Thus, we will truly become his followers and be worthy to bear the name of Christians acting mercifully toward all whom we meet. We will become the forgiving love of God in Jesus, released by their Spirit of love and extended on this earth as we enflesh the merciful Jesus before others, who, perhaps, have not yet heard the Good News of God as forgiving mercy to all his children in their brokenness.

CHAPTER SIX

Jesus — God's Mercy Revealed

Elie Wiesel, a Jewish survivor of Auschwitz, in his novel, *Night*, gives us a powerful description of the question all of us constantly ask: "Where is God now?":

> The SS hanged two Jewish men and a youth in front of the whole camp. The men died quickly, but the death throes of the youth lasted for half an hour. 'Where is God? Where is he?' someone asked behind me. As the youth still hung in torment in the noose after a long time, I heard the man call again, 'Where is God now?' And I heard a voice in myself answer: 'Where is he? He is here. He is hanging there on the gallows. . . .' (*Night*, p. 75).

Where is God to be seen as mercy, self-emptying love come down to us in our miseries and brokenness to lift us up to new life? The most basic truth upon which we Christians build our faith is that God has unveiled for us in his only begotten Son, made flesh, his very own essence as love and mercy shown toward us.

A Sufi proverb says:

> What the sun is,
> Only the sun can teach us.
> He who would learn
> must towards it turn.

How can we come to know God's mercy, except that God's Word made flesh reveals to us in human words and actions that God is constantly merciful toward us, unless we turn to his incarnate Word, Jesus Christ? God so loves us as to give us his only begotten Son so that whoever believes he is the true image of the Heavenly Father, will be healed and made whole (Jn 3:16).

Through the faith, hope and love infused into us by the Spirit of the risen Jesus, we can accept the revelations made to us by him in his historical life on earth as recorded in the New Testament and explicated by his Church. We do not have to conjure up ideas of what God is truly like, especially in regard to his constant mercy toward us. We ground our faith in the historical person of Jesus Christ, and the unbelievable Good News that he is truly the Son of God from all eternity, of one substance with the Father who for love of us, freely became one of us.

The incarnation, when God's Word pitched his tent among us by becoming totally human, as well as being totally divine by nature, is God's wonderful plan to reveal his loving mercy to us in the historical actions of Jesus Christ. "To have seen me is to have seen the Father" (Jn 14:9). We now have the Way, the Truth and the Life (Jn 14:6): Jesus Christ who leads us to the unseen God.

Contemplating God's Image In Christ

BY THE POWER of the Holy Spirit, we can believe that this historical person, Jesus of Nazareth, born of a woman (Gal 4:5), is the exact image of the mercy of our Heavenly Father. God acts as Jesus acted. His teachings about mercy, as recorded in the New Testament, give us an objectivity that is bestowed through faith as a gift of his Spirit, that surpasses any human knowledge acquired by our own human intellect.

However, an image often implies an exact duplicate, a static reproduction, as an image in a mirror reproduces an exact picture of the person who stands before it. It is necessary to contemplate prayerfully the life and actions of Jesus through the illumination of the Holy Spirit. We turn prayerfully to Jesus' teachings on mercy, especially in his parables, in order to be grounded in God's living Word that is Truth.

Contemplating God's mercy as revealed in the Gospels, brings us to an ever-increasing awareness of Christ's resurrectional presence living within us individually and within his body, the Church. Allowing him to unveil God's mercy to us in the context of our human situation of each moment, we commit ourselves in obedience to his continued revelation as found in Scripture, but as discovered in our intimate oneness with the risen Lord. It is this living in the mercy of God revealed in our daily brokenness by the risen Jesus who has suffered and died "for me," as St. Paul discovered

(Gal 2:20), that will transform us into compassionate, merciful persons toward all whom we meet and serve.

A Compassionate Suffering Servant

Jesus, the radiant Light (Heb 1:3) of the reflected glory of the Father from all eternity, consented to assume the condition of Adam, and all humanity, who by sin became slaves to their own selves. Jesus, however, did not hold on selfishly to his divine nature, but, precisely because he was divine, he surrendered that powerful divine nature in loving, merciful self-sacrifice on our behalf (Ph 2:6-11).

To reveal to us God's true nature as merciful love, Jesus takes on the form of a suffering, compassionate, merciful servant, he enters into our darkened world. He is tempted in all things, save sin (Heb 4:15). He consents, not to claim his natural, divine right to rule over the world, but to gain it from his Father by merciful, humble love for us unto his death on the cross, Jesus not only teaches the world, but he lives out this basic truth that possessiveness of life, things, other persons, and even of God, destroys while only true love manifested in total self-giving heals, liberates and brings happiness that will last forever.

Such is the way of the merciful Jesus. But it is his way and his life only because it is the same as that of his Father. How could both persons, being equally God by nature, be anything other than love by nature, by their very being? And such love by nature must be self-sacrificing on behalf of the broken ones with whom God wishes to share in his divine life. Jesus is mercy, the Father is mercy, and the Holy Spirit is mercy. All manifest, uniquely, the same nature of God, who is always merciful love, living always to serve the happiness of others.

This triune God loves us with a passion, the very passion of Jesus. In Jesus' total submission to the point where he possesses nothing of his own to prove his love for us, Jesus shows us the Father's infinite love for each of us. "As the Father has loved me, so I have loved you" (Jn 15:9).

When Jesus became a weak child, he was unveiling the weakness of God, ready to dispossess himself of his life in order to show mercy and forgiveness, so that he might share that life totally with us. God's weakness is the power he places into our hands to call him Father. We can hurt him, just as Jesus submitted to hurts and rejections when he offered his love to human beings and received abuse and indifference. We can reject his mercy whenever we fail to be merciful toward others as Jesus is toward us.

The Merciful Jesus

JESUS PURSUED the sinners, the outcasts of society, the maimed, the lepers, in a word, those most sunken into miseries from which they could not extricate themselves. He drove out the evil spirits of despondency and loneliness by his involving, merciful self-giving to the broken ones of this earth. He tenderly touched the lepers, the paralytics, the blind and the lame and gave them new life through the mercy he showed them. He entered into the brokenness of human miseries and mercifully became a sharing part of such brokenness. The evils of the physical and moral orders surrounded him from all sides. Such darkness dragged him deeper and deeper into its darkness like quicksand. Jesus entered into the dregs of society "to be made sin for us" (2 Cor 5:21).

The broken ones of this earth to whom other human beings showed no mercy, clawed at him. As soon as he looked for rest in order to escape from human brokenness, in order to be one with the wholeness of his Father, they brought him more of the diseased to be healed. Jesus touched human evils because he was the exact image of the Father who never turns away from us, his children, immersed so deeply in miseries.

Jesus stretched out his healing hands and the sick felt the love of God pour into their broken bodies, minds and hearts. He was the Son of God and for a brief moment they hung suspended between the darkness of their now isolation and the light of the truth that they too were sons and daughters of God. They yielded to the presence of Jesus' merciful love in their lives and they felt wholeness come over them. It is only merciful love that heals and transforms us from our brokenness and miseries into loving, merciful servants toward others.

Jesus Experienced The Father's Mercy

THE DIVINE WORD, one with the Father from all eternity, and one with the perfect loving Holy Spirit, could never have experienced mercy since he possessed no brokenness, no misery, no "not-yetness." But the amazing element of the incarnation, when God's Word became enfleshed and became both divine and human in one person, who was both God and man, is that now God can experience mercy in Jesus Christ. God no longer stood outside of creatureliness and sin. God threw himself into the midst of sin for our sakes.

In his human frailty, as he was tempted in all things, Jesus, in his human "otherness," from God's perfect holiness, in a continued process all his earthly life, experienced the merciful love of his Heavenly Father. In his experiences, Jesus, especially in his temptations, had to discover and manifest the Spirit that belongs to him whom he possesses as his very own Spirit. Jesus was driven into the desert by the Holy Spirit (Mk 1:12) and there he was tempted. He was tempted all his lifetime like us in all things, save sin (Heb 4:15). Jesus was sinless because he yielded to God's Spirit within himself and went against any urge toward independence.

Overwhelmed in the desert temptations and, even more so, in his temptations in Gethsemane and on the cross on Calvary (intense moments of entering into brokenness and doing the inner battle, are but symbols of a lifetime of struggles), Jesus had to turn within himself. There, in the Spirit, he discovered the self-emptying, merciful love of his Heavenly Father. Imaging the Father's holiness in his own human development, Jesus grew as man in each event as he sought humbly to do, not his own, but his Father's will (Heb 10:9).

He learned to become merciful toward the broken ones of this earth because he daily discovered the outpoured mercy of the Father for him. Especially in his greatest temptations on the cross as he underwent agonizing sufferings and approaching death, he must have had to struggle to search for the merciful love of the Father in the darkness of seeming abandonment by the Father. Yet, in spite of his temptations, Jesus pushed to new depths of holiness and loving surrender: he cried out for the mercy of his Abba!

Only because Jesus, throughout his lifetime, strove to experience the Father's immense mercy toward him, as revealed by the Spirit of love, was he in his human consciousness transformed to become a merciful healing Savior to the broken ones who came to him for healing.

Jesus Teaches Mercy

JESUS CHRIST, God become man for love of us, came among us as a light that shines in our darkness of sin and brokenness, "a light that shines in the dark, a light that darkness could not overpower" (Jn 1:4-5). He is God's living Word sent to us in human form to communicate to us all we need to know about God's nature, our human destiny and the purpose of God's creation. Jesus is more than a prophet, given a mandate to speak on behalf of God who anoints such a communicator. Jesus is the medium of God's revelation to us, but above all, he *is* the message. He is the living Word of God who cannot deceive nor be deceived.

If we obey his words by acting on them, an amazing work of divinizing us takes place through the immanent indwelling of the Trinity. "If anyone loves me, he will keep my word, and my Father will love him, and we shall come to him and make our home in him. Those who do not love me do not keep my words. And my word is not my own: it is the word of the one who sent me" (Jn 14:23-24).

Jesus' teachings are predominantly presented in the Synoptic Gospels of Mark, Matthew and Luke in the form of parables. The Gospel parables are a unique development of a literary form having its roots in Old Testament and rabbinic literature. Jesus sets forth his teachings in such wise sayings or fictitious short stories.

In his beautifully simple stories, Jesus gives us sublime teachings about his Father's mercy toward all of us, his children. Jesus lived and taught one revealed truth: how great is the Trinity's love — Father, Son and Holy Spirit — for us, created in God's image and likeness. In John's Gospel, Jesus says: ". . . The Father himself loves you for loving me and believing that I came from God. I came from the Father and have come into the world and now I leave the world to go to the Father" (Jn 16:27-28). Whether he is describing himself or teaching us about his Father's mercy toward us, what applies to Jesus, the Word incarnate (and, hence, the importance of believing that he came from God and is truly God), applies also to the Father in his merciful actions toward his children.

God is a Good Shepherd in the person of Jesus Christ. He leaves the ninety-nine righteous ones (or those who consider themselves already saved!) and searches out the one lost sheep. He joyfully carries the sheep on his shoulders and, on returning home, calls his friends to celebrate with joy the finding of the lost sheep (Lk 15:4-7).

God searches out with great diligence the lost person, much as a woman with ten drachmas searches out the one she has lost. Again, she, too, rejoices with her friends at having found the lost drachma. Again, the point Jesus is revealing to us is: "In the same way, I tell you, there is rejoicing among the angels of God over one repentant sinner" (Lk 15:8-10).

The Prodigal Father

ST. LUKE'S GOSPEL is one that highlights the mercy of God, especially in his series of parables. No doubt, the most well-known and favorite story in all of the Old and New Testament teachings about the Heavenly Father's forgiving mercy is the story Luke tells about the lost prodigal son. It is a dramatic presentation given by Jesus to the tax collectors and the sinners to illustrate the great Heavenly mercy of his Father. This drama has three "actors": the father, who represents the Heavenly Father; the younger son, who leaves home after demanding all his inheritance. Having lost all on "riotous living," he sits feeding the swine and comes to a conversion. He arises and returns to his loving father and humbly asks forgiveness for his having left home and having rejected the father's love for him. The third actor, the elder son, stands for the righteous one of Israel who observed all the commands of his father, but who had no love for him nor for their own brethren (Lk 15:11-32).

Scriptural exegetes stress the setting in which Jesus delivers this parable. Jesus is seeking to instruct the Pharisees and the scribes on why he welcomes the tax collectors and sinners and even eats with them. Jesus' merciful fellowship with sinners is an image of how the Heavenly Father goes out to the broken ones of this earth and offers forgiveness and mercy.

But, the details of the loving father toward both the elder son, who does not leave home (a symbol of the Jews who observed all the legal details of the Old Testament), and his relationship of forgiving love toward his wayward, younger son often are highlighted, much to the neglect of the important story of the father, symbol of the Heavenly Father, in the way he forgives his sinful children.

It would be difficult for us to understand the tremendous statement Jesus was making about his Heavenly Father and the type of mercy he shows to repentant sinners. Jewish families were built up on the patriarchal model with the father of the family as almost an autocrat, ruling with dispassionate power. It must have shocked his listeners as Jesus told them of their Heavenly Father, unlike the patriarchal father of a Jewish family. This Father truly waits with great patience for the return of his ungrateful son. Daily he scans the horizon, eagerly hoping to catch a glimpse of the returned son.

When he sees his son returning, but still a long way off, the father, stirred to pity, forgets his hurt pride and patriarchal dignity and runs toward his son. He runs and thows his arms round his son's neck and "kisses him affectionately" (Lk 15:20). There are two great and explicit teachings that reveal what our Heavenly Father's relationships toward us are like.

The first truth that Jesus reveals to us is that we can impact the very life of God. In the parable, we see how the father waits with sadness in his heart for the return of his sinful son. Then, upon seeing him return in repentance, the aged father throws aside all his dignity and honor and runs with compassion to embrace the son. The Good News Jesus brings us is that the Heavenly Father truly rejoices as he shows us mercy in our repentance. His heart dances with joy along with all the angels in Heaven when one of his children repents and returns home!

The second truth is that the Heavenly Father is not only the almighty God, Creator of heaven and earth, the *animus*, powerful in intellect, since he knows all things, omnipotent, since he is the Source of all being and can do what is impossible for his creatures. The Father of Jesus is a waiting, merciful, loving God. It is somewhat the love of a mother, full of affection, ready to suffer and weep for her children. Jesus imaged such a Father when he wept over Jerusalem (Lk 19:41). "How often have I longed to gather your children, as a hen gathers her brood under wings, and you refused!" (Lk 13:34; Mt 23:37).

A Waiting God

DOES GOD really wait for our return to him as this parable shows? How can God, who is perfect, independent of all his creatures, and, therefore, immutable, be affected by us? Can God really relate to us in true relationships? St. Thomas Aquinas in the 13th century taught that God in his complete transcendence cannot have a *real* relationship with us creatures, since Thomas taught that would make God depend upon his own creatures to supply some attributes which he did not always possess in his absolute transcendent perfection from all eternity (*Summa Theologiae*: I, 13, 7 ad 4).

Yet, both the Old and New Testaments show that God is a God of *pathos*. Above all, in Jesus Christ we see clearly that God, yes, in his essence, is immutable and perfect. But the triune God freely chooses to burst forth in self-emptying love through his uncreated energies of love to be the intimate Ground of all creatures' being. God is transcendent and absolute subsistence in himself, yet, through his free will, he has chosen to be supremely *relative* to his created world. He did not have to create us or the material world. He freely creates our world and sees it to be very good (Gn 1:31). He, therefore, freely wills to enter into a love relationship with his human children, giving and receiving love from us.

God gives created beings their "otherness," yet he also wants to receive a return of love from them. God is eternal, but also active and receptive in creation and redemption. He is impassible, but also "passable." He is the "inside," immanent ground of all beings, but is not dependent upon creatures to complete himself in his essence or nature.

Jesus reveals in his teachings and actions, as the perfect image of the Father, that God's eternal, perfect nature as self-emptying love within the Trinity freely calls out for a complementary self-giving to the created world in which he becomes the "insideness" of its very being. God freely chooses to share his loving, triune community with us rational creatures by surrendering his self-sufficiency and independence and by waiting upon us in whom he resides as our source of existence.

God respects our freedom, as the father in this parable respects his sons, and, therefore, he does not coerce us. He offers his self-gift to "entice," or "allure," us to return his gift of love. Love within the Trinity and toward us, his creatures, is not only self-giving to the "other." True love waits to receive uniqueness as a gift from the self-emptying love of another. As Gabriel Marcel writes: "The *I* is the child of the *We*."

Love Differentiates As It Unites

JESUS REVEALS that perfect love within the Trinity is circular. The Father is eternally becoming Father through giving himself in his Spirit of love to the Son who is begotten in that gift. God's Word eternally receives being from the eternal Mind, the Father. He eternally returns that gift by becoming a gift to the waiting Father through the same Spirit of love. The uniqueness of the Father comes only in the completion of an eternal giving and an eternally receiving of his uniqueness toward and from his Son in the same Spirit.

Jesus Christ, God-Man, continues that process of trinitarian unity and uniqueness, even in his earthly life. Through human actions, e.g., being baptized by John the Baptist in the river Jordan, Jesus delighted, in time and space on this earth, the eternal Father. Jesus heard the Father speak these words: "You are my Son, the Beloved; my favor rests on you" (Lk 3:22).

When we in our sinfulness call out to Jesus, God-Man, to have mercy on us, we can experience God's forgiving love through Jesus' sufferings and death for each of us. We can return God's love in and with Jesus as our Head and as we, his members, seek to delight, to thrill, the heart of the Heavenly Father. Truly, he rejoices because the total Christ is being formed. Jesus Christ, risen and in glory, is united by the Spirit to his repentant and divinized members. In him and, yet, with our unique gift freely given to the Father, we can return the Father's love, which he manifests in Christ. But, we can only thrill the Father's heart and make him rejoice as the father in the parable rejoiced when he sees us becoming in his Word made flesh, Jesus Christ, a part of him, capable in his Spirit to call out with Jesus: "Abba!" (Rm 8:15; Gal 4:7).

Jesus Acts Mercifully As The Father Does

As we have pointed out, Jesus progressively, through temptations and trials, experienced the mercy of the Father toward him in his human frailties. As he experienced himself as being loved infinitely by his Heavenly Father, so he became more and more the human image of God's love toward all whom he encountered in his public life. On every page of the Gospels, we find Jesus acting mercifully toward the needy.

We need to contemplate prayerfully Jesus in his merciful actions in order to believe that the Heavenly Father, not in actions of mercy that begin and end, but by his very nature as love, likewise, is always showing us mercy in his condescending compassion and forgiving love.

Jesus' first believers had seen Jesus, filled with the compassion of a mother for her suffering children, with the protective love of a shepherd for his sheep, with the total self-giving of a bridegroom for his bride, heal the multitude of sick persons brought to him.

> He went round the whole of Galilee teaching in their synagogues, proclaiming the Good News of the kingdom and curing all kinds of diseases and sickness among the people (Mt 4:23-24).

> His fame spread throughout Syria, and those who were suffering from diseases and painful complaints of one kind or another, the possessed epileptics, the paralyzed, were brought to him and he cured them (Mt 9:35). He summoned his twelve disciples, and gave them authority over unclean spirits with power to cast them out and to cure all kinds of diseases and sickness (Mt 10:1).

With what compassion Jesus raised the dead son of the widow of Naim and returned him to the suffering mother! (Lk 7:11-17). He had mercy on the woman with the issue of blood from which she suffered for twelve years and healed her (Lk 8:40-48). He raised Jairus' daughter from the dead out of mercy toward her grieving parents (Lk 8:40-56). He cured the centurion's servant at a distance because he admired the centurion's faith (Lk 7:1-10).

To the sinful woman, who anointed him while he dined at the home of Simon the Pharisee, Jesus showed mercy and forgave her sins. Much was forgiven her because she loved much. Simon had only contempt for her as a public sinner; hence he was not forgiven much for his lack of great love. Jesus showed mercy and compassion on the multitudes that followed him into the desert by multiplying the loaves and fishes to feed them (Lk 9:10-17; Mt 14:13-21; Mk 6:30-44; Jn 6:1-13).

He shows mercy by healing the Gerasene demoniac (Lk 8:26-39), as well as the epileptic demoniac through the petition of his father (Lk 9:37-43). He cleansed the ten lepers out of mercy for them. He had mercy on the crippled woman who suffered for 18 years and healed her on the Sabbath to show that the Heavenly Father always works and cannot be stopped from bringing mercy and healing to his children, not even on the Sabbath (Lk 13:10-17).

How touching and with a bit of humor Jesus stopped before the sycamore tree in which the small Zacchaeus, the publican, was hiding in order to see Jesus as he passed. Jesus invited himself to go to his home to bring salvation to him, as he repents of his crime in cheating others, and to his entire family (Lk 19:1-10). For this is why the Son of Man had come: to seek out and save what was lost.

Fullness Of Mercy On the Cross

BUT the greatest revelation of God's mercy is given us as we stand at the foot of the cross and contemplate Jesus' merciful actions and his death itself as the climax of God's revelation of perfect mercy toward us. Before he died, Jesus forgave his persecutors: "Father, forgive them; they do not know what they are doing" (Lk 23:24). Turning to the good thief on his right, who begged Jesus to remember him in his Kingdom, Jesus promised him with the mercy of his Heavenly Father to all repentant sinners, no matter how great their sins: "Indeed, I promise you, today you will be with me in paradise" (Lk 23:43).

We contemplate the terrifying sufferings, the extreme darkness of complete rejection and abandonment that Jesus underwent on the cross and in his final moments before death. We do not formulate with logic what it cost God in the sufferings and death of Jesus to manifest his infinite mercy toward us. Such knowledge can be attained only as an intuition granted to the *anawim*, the poor in spirit, the little ones in God's kingdom, who are not scandalized by God's self-emptying love in such weakness. "For God's foolishness is wiser than human wisdom, and God's weakness is stronger than human strength" (1 Cor 1:25).

Nowhere is God more revealed as God, whose very nature is love, than in the revelation of Jesus, broken and rejected, as Mercy itself poured out on the cross to the last drop of blood! In the self-emptying and total surrender of Jesus to his Father on our behalf, we are at last able to enter into the trinitarian community and there discover that God's mercy toward us is above all his works. God's great love for us (Jn 3:16) can only be seen perfectly mirrored by the crucified Jesus. He is the image of the invisible God (Col 1:15), the concrete, human expression of what continually occurs within the Trinity in their merciful actions toward us.

God's Essence Is Mercy

As we humbly stand at the foot of the cross, we can receive the Good News through the Spirit poured forth as Living Water from Jesus's innermost being (Jn 7:38). In deep faith, hope and love, we realize that Jesus' greatest act of mercy is also the image of God's very own essence as mercy. Although Jesus suffered and died only once out of mercy for us to save and heal us from our miseries, yet, as God the Son, one with the Father and the Holy Spirit, he is always mercy toward us.

Jesus makes possible, by his Spirit, our realization that his mercy is not an attribute God demonstrates by doing merciful acts and then stops acting mercifully. God *is* mercy in his very being as perfect and absolute transcendent Beauty. God, unlike us, does not *begin* to show us his condescending mercy in any given action that then may come to an end. We cry out for his mercy. But never do we need to beg or cajole God to do something he is not always *doing*. His *being* is his *action*. He is mercy! He is always acting mercifully toward us.

But it is really we who need to come to God in repentance, as the prodigal son returned to his father and to experience God's constant state of being love, holy, merciful and forgiving. That is why contemplating Christ on the cross is more than a return in our memory to a hill outside of

Jerusalem. Through his resurrection from the dead and the outpouring of his Spirit, we can now, through the powerful high-priestly intercession of Jesus, stand before Jesus crucified, he who *is* God's mercy.

We need not cry out for God's mercy to ask him to give us his mercy. But we do need to come in repentance before God's perfect and total mercy, always manifested to us by Jesus crucified and risen from the dead.

Come To Me All Who Are Burdened

WE DO NOT NEED to ask for God's mercy. If God exists, he exists as mercy. He exists unceasingly as merciful action toward us. It is for us to come into his merciful presence and surrender to his forgiving mercy. It is for us to believe in Jesus Christ, as the Son of God, who freely died to take away our sins, and revealed God's nature as mercy. It is not enough that we believe God is merciful. We must believe in Jesus Christ, the full manifestation of God's state of continual mercy toward us.

God *is* on-going manifestation to each of us as Love, perfect in self-surrendering unto death to touch each of us by his nature as mercy for us in our miseries. "A man can have no greater love than to lay down his life for his friends" (Jn 15:13). We might also add: "Nor can God!" God reaches the peak of speaking his Word in Jesus Christ. He can be no more present as mercy than in his image, Jesus, who poured himself out on the cross, even to the last drop of blood. He was made sin, rejected and outcast to become one with us in our brokenness.

How can we continue to disbelieve in God's perfect mercy toward us? How can we refuse to bring to him through Jesus all our guilt and fears, past sins and dark brokenness, worries and anxieties and accept his ready mercy that alone can heal us and make us holy? The secret is to believe Jesus Christ is truly God's mercy in human form. We can do nothing to "merit" God's mercy. It is God's gift. But God *is* the Gift! God's mercy is God!

We make contact with God as mercy through the revelation of Jesus as burning, active, concerned love coming down into our miseries to share our brokenness in order that in God's forgiving mercy, we can be transformed into the beautiful children God has predestined us to be in Jesus Christ.

St. Paul eloquently expresses the mystery of God's mercy toward us, gratuitously given, without our asking him to be our mercy:

> But God, who is rich in mercy,
> was moved by the intense love with which he loved us,
> and when we were dead by reason of our transgressions,
> he made us live with the life of Christ.
> By grace you have been saved.
> Together with Christ Jesus and in him,
> he raised us up and enthroned us in the heavenly realm,
> that in Christ Jesus he might show throughout the ages
>   to come the overflowing riches of his grace
> springing from his goodness to us.
> Yes, it is by grace that you have been saved through faith;
> it is the gift of God;
> it is not the result of anything you did,
> so that no one has any grounds for boasting.
> We are his handiwork,
> created in Christ Jesus in view of good deeds
> which God prepared beforehand for us to practice
>   (Ep 2:4-10).

God has bound himself to be mercy, absolute and inexhaustible, toward us. He cannot be unfaithful to himself for his very nature is to be mercy toward us. "Though we be faithless, he remains faithful, since he cannot disown himself" (2 Tm 2:13).

It is for us to accept God in Jesus Christ and be transformed into loving merciful persons toward others.

Happy the merciful: they shall have mercy shown them (Mt 5:7).

CHAPTER SEVEN

Be Merciful As Your Father Is Merciful

This is a book primarily about the infinite, loving mercy of God toward us human beings. Yet, we cannot merely dwell on God's mercy without speaking about the mercy we need to show toward our neighbors, toward everyman and woman created, toward each human being as our brother or sister.

Too often preachers and spiritual writers exhort us to imitate God in his active love toward us. As God loves us, we are told, so we are to love each other. It is the second commandment Jesus preached: that we are to love others as we love ourselves. Yet, so rarely are we exhorted to the middle stage between our receiving God's mercy and showing mercy to others. That middle stage consists in our being transformed into beautiful persons as we experience and accept God's infinite mercy. We are to act always mercifully since we have been changed by God's mercy into persons who have *become* mercy by God's constant, loving mercy toward them.

The inconsistency of receiving God's mercy and not showing such loving mercy to others is highlighted in St. John's First Epistle:

> If anyone says, "My love is fixed on God,"
> yet hates his brother,
> he is a liar.
> One who has no love for the brother he has seen
> cannot love the God he has not seen.
> The commandment we have from him is this:
> whoever loves God must also love his brother (1 Jn 4:20-21).

The Qualities Of Mercy

AS WE RELATE to God, so we relate to other human beings. And, as we relate to other human beings, to that degree we relate to God. St. James writes: "Merciless is the judgment on the man who has not shown mercy; but mercy triumphs over judgment" (Jm 2:13). But this is the basic teaching of Jesus himself: "Blest are they who show mercy; mercy shall be theirs" (Mt 5:7).

Shakespeare eloquently praises the qualities, both of God's mercy and our own human mercy shown to others. It is the true, earthly mercy shown to others. It is the true earthly power that best shows ourselves most like God.

The quality of mercy is not strain'd,
It droppeth as the gentle rain from heaven
Upon the place beneath; it is twice blest;
It blesseth him that gives, and him that takes;
'Tis mightiest in the mightiest; it becomes
The throned monarch better than his crown;
His sceptre shows the force of temporal power,
the attribute to awe and majesty,
wherein doth sit the fear and dread of Kings;
But mercy is above this sceptred sway;
It is enthroned in the hearts of Kings;
It is an attribute to God Himself;
And earthly power doth then show likest God's
When mercy seasons justice. Therefore, Jew,
Though justice be thy plea, consider this,
That, in the course of justice, none of us
Should see salvation: we do pray for mercy;
And that same prayer doth teach us all to render
The deeds of mercy (*The Merchant of Venice*; Act 4, Sc 1).

Mercy — Love In Action

ST. THOMAS AQUINAS shows that the perfection of God and ourselves, as reflected in our spiritual life, is seen in love or charity. St. Paul tells us that the greatest of all virtues or power on earth and in heaven is charity or love: "... and the greatest of these is love" (1 Cor 13:13). We could say that love is the root and mercy is the fruit-bearing tree. Mercy is the acting out of love given by God or ourselves to someone in need.

The fruitful tree cannot be fruitful unless it is one with the roots that feed the tree with life. Love is the greatest. Yet, it needs merciful acts shown to persons in their concrete needs in order to be actuated love. Love cannot remain invisible, unexpressed, not acted out in merciful acts. Love dies, unless it explodes outward, and in merciful deeds becomes incarnate, enfleshed in a loving sacrifice given to another.

St. James shows us that faith without good works is dead: "Be assured, then that faith without works is as dead as a body without breath" (Ja 2:26). Christ brings us a new commandment: to love others even as he loves us. This builds on the universal commandment, known intuitively by every human being, to show love to one's neighbor and every human person is that neighbor.

Jesus tells all who wish to be his disciples: "A new commandment I give to you, that you love one another: that as I have loved you, you also love one another. By this will all men know that you are my disciples, if you have love for one another" (Jn 13:34-35). He not only preached that the Father loves us with a merciful love of infinite concern and forgiveness, but he, the image of the Father's love and mercy (Jn 14:9), also acted out this involving, active love, in his merciful acts toward all whom he met.

Pope St. Gregory the Great summarized the relation of good works and love: "Our Lord's precepts are many, yet only one; many by diversity of work, and only one in the root of love." We can act merciful in a consistent way only if we abide in the love and power of Jesus (Jn 15:4).

Love Your Enemies

BUT, if Christ abides in us and we abide in him, as branches that receive life from the root of the vine (Jn 15:5), we will bear great fruit. St. Luke's Gospel, the "social" Gospel, spells out in concrete examples what love in merciful actions means. It is a description of what a true Christian looks like in action toward others.

> Love your enemies; do good to those who hate you; bless those who curse you and pray for those who maltreat you. When someone slaps you on one cheek, turn and give him the other; when someone takes your coat, let him have your shirt as well. Give to all who beg from you. When a man takes what is yours, do not demand it back. Do to others what you would have them do to you. If you love those who love you, what credit is that to you? Even sinners love those who love them. If you do good to those who do good to you, how can you claim any credit? Sinners do as much. If you lend to those from whom you expect repayment, what merit is there in it for you? Even sinners lend to sinners, expecting to be repaid in full.
>
> Love your enemy and do good; lend without expecting repayment. Then will your recompense be great. You will rightly be called sons of the Most High, since he himself is good to the ungrateful and the wicked.
>
> Be compassionate, as your Father is compassionate. Do not judge, and you will not be judged. Do not condemn, and you will not be condemned. Pardon, and you shall be pardoned. Give, and it shall be given to you. Good measure pressed down, shaken together, running over, will they pour into the fold of your garment. For the measure you measure with will be measured back to you (Lk 6:27-38).

Mercy And Justice

ST. THOMAS beautifully defines mercy as, "A heart suffering over the sufferings of others." He undoubtedly was inspired by the Latin word for mercy: *misericordia*. Mercy is two hearts meeting in sadness or compassion, a mutual suffering over the misery or sufferings of another.

We can see that mercy goes far beyond justice. True charity, that is built upon the hope we have in the beautiful unique person of the other, in spite of externals and actions that seem to cover over the godly in the other, must be built on justice. Justice flows out of God's unique love for each human person. Each of us has been created with a special place in the heart of God, who calls us to a unique place in time in the Body of his Son, Jesus Christ.

In this vale of tears, there will always be the poor, the oppressed, the biblical *amharez*, the landed people, forced to live off the land, but who can never call any land their own. Thus, true mercy or love in action must be prompted by justice to strive to establish the dignity of each human person. The Book of Proverbs succinctly calls us to God's preference for the poor: "He that has mercy on the poor, lends to the Lord; and he will repay him" (Pr 19:17).

Surely this is nothing but the teaching of Jesus:

> ... I was hungry and you gave me food; I was thirsty and you gave me drink; I was a stranger and you made me welcome; naked and you clothed me; sick and you visited me; in prison, and you came to see me. Then the virtuous will say to him in reply, 'Lord, when did we see you hungry and feed you; or thirsty and give you drink? When did we

see you a stranger and make you welcome; naked, and clothe you; sick or in prison and go to see you?' And the King will answer, 'I tell you solemnly, insofar as you did this to one of the least of these brothers of mine, you did it to me' (Mt 25:35-40).

Involving Mercy

HERE we have the ultimate purpose of why we show mercy to the needy on any level of physical, psychical or spiritual impoverishment by our corporal and spiritual works. Our motive is not to merit a heavenly reward in the next life. It is, rather, to build up the Body of Christ through "filling up the sufferings of Christ" that come from our actively showing mercy to every man and woman, cost what it may for us in terms of personal sacrifices.

The disciples of Jesus learned from his teachings and his personal life that to have a part with him, they had to deny their self-centered isolation. They had to embrace the cross of sufferings that would accompany the movement of living actively to serve the needs of others.

The Apostles and the early Christians never failed to emphasize Jesus' teaching, that, whatsoever we would do to the least of those around us, we would be doing to him. The *Acts of the Apostles* are filled with the merciful acts that Christians performed toward the sick and the poor and the suffering of any kind. The early followers of Jesus were filled with the mercy of God shown by Jesus, Mercy incarnate, to them individually, and as a community. They knew such generosity transformed them into loving, caring persons and communities that shared everything in common with those who were in need.

We read in the *Acts*: "and the disciples, every man according to his ability, purposed to send relief to the brethren who dwelt in Judea, which also they did, sending it to the ancients by the hands of Barnabas and Saul" (Ac 11:29-30). This was at the time of the famine in the reign of Emperor Claudius. St. Paul declared: "Now after several years I came to bring alms to my nation" (Ac 24:17).

Organized Charity

THOSE in the early Church, who had a greater share of this earth's goods gave generously to help out others in countries hit by famine and drought. It was a generous charity, well-organized as we see from the establishment of the orders of deacons and deaconesses to distribute goods to the needy.

We see that when the Greek converts in Jerusalem complained to the Jewish Christians that their widows were being neglected, deacons were appointed to look after the poor. Thus, seven men of good reputation were chosen to see to the distribution of food, clothing, etc. to take care of the needy. Deaconesses were appointed to work among the women of the community. These assisted in the baptism of women, gave them instruction, and visited the sick and the imprisoned.

St. Paul's writings show him to be the apostle of mercy and charity to all who were in need. He was continually concerned about taking up collections for the poor, urging hospitality to strangers, practising compassion toward the imprisoned, standing up for the enslaved, exercising fraternal correction. Every work of mercy spiritual or corporal, can be found in his admonitions.

For this reason, St. John Chrysostom reminds us: "Let us make St. Paul mount into this holy pulpit with us, that great procurator of all the poor; there is not one of his epistles where he does not recommend the poor. He knew how important was this duty."

Sharing God's Gifts With The Needy

IT WAS the Christian conviction that if anyone had riches from God, it was his or her duty to distribute them as stewards of God's gifts. Christians were to consider themselves God's treasurers or faithful stewards, and they did not consider it an extraordinary task. Their lives were simple, their wants were few. They scorned luxury and unnecessary comforts. Luxury was for the pagans who knew not Christ. We find Fathers, such as Clement and Cyprian, condemning the all too luxurious lives of the pagans.

In the post-apostolic times in which we are now living, we Christians should know that once our simple wants are provided for, it is our Christian duty to give of our superfluity, great or little, to the poor. At liturgical gatherings on Sunday and feast days, at the time of the first reading, the early Christians placed their gifts of money or food on the altar, as their personal gifts to God. Also, there were chests in the Church for their offerings.

The gifts offered during the liturgical meetings or those placed in appropriate chests, included the proceeds also from property which some Christians voluntarily sold, or rent collected on leased-out property. These were given to the bishop who in turn distributed them through deacons, subdeacons and deaconesses. By this method of secret distribution, the self-respect of the poor was protected.

There was no room for chance begging or idleness. Only the deserving poor were helped. In return, recipients were expected to pray for their donors. This process was a necessary one, considering the times in which they lived, especially the continual persecutions. Christians then constituted a race apart, pariahs, suspected of being enemies of the state. They were calumniated and persecuted and faced martyrdom every day.

Many believed that the end of the world was imminent. They minimized daily life that brought much sacrifice and pain. They spent time in prayer and fasting. They knew there was no sense in piling up worldly wealth, while their brothers and sisters suffered in misery. To live poorly was considered a blessing, something to strive toward. To share with one another was just a part of daily life, the way God intended us to live in Christ. The brotherly aid included all works of mercy, not only to their Christian brethren, who lived afar, but even to pagans. The Christian community was open to the universal brotherhood of all men and women, all children of the same Heavenly Father.

For this reason, St. Ambrose could write: "If you give to a poor man, you do not share with him what belongs to you, but you return to him what is his. For you have usurped what was given for the common use of all." St. Gregory the Great echoes the same understanding: "When we minister some necessary things to the needy, we do not give them what is ours, but we give them back what is theirs, thus, complying with an obligation of justice, rather than performing a work of mercy."

Right Of Wealth

JESUS did not condemn wealth in itself, but only the mammon of iniquity, riches in surplus. He even said wealth could be used to lay up treasures in Heaven. It also often could be an occasion, however, of moral destruction. But, when used aright, it could be the source of many spiritual blessings. St. Augustine writes: "Let the rich use what their infirmity has accustomed them to; but let them be sorry that they are not able to do otherwise. For it would be better for them if they could." He says that St. Paul "reprehends the desire after riches only, not the proper use of them."

During the last century, Pope Leo XIII taught, "Money and the other things which men call good and desirable, we may have them in abundance, or we may want them altogether; as far as eternal happiness is concerned, it is no matter; the only thing that is important is to use them aright." If there were no wealth, there would be no alms to give those in need.

The early Fathers drew out practical applications of giving alms and sharing one's wealth with those in need in a universal teaching. St. Augustine writes, "Mercy is the compassion in our hearts of another's misery, by which, if we can, we are compelled to alleviate it." The Fathers called almsgiving "another baptism." St. Jerome insists; "Such alms cleanse the soul as by an immersion; the fire of hell is extinguished by the sacred font, and the worm of conscience is destroyed by the pious liberality which relieves Christ in the poor."

Why Practice Works Of Mercy?

THE EARLY TEACHERS, who exhorted Christians to practice works of mercy and whose teachings we have received and hopefully practice also, based their exhortations on the example of Christ and his teachings. Christ, the Son of God, brought a completely new element to our practice of mercy toward others in need. For he, by our belief *in* him as the true Son of God, God from God, came to reveal the fullness of God's mercy toward all human beings. In his perfect act of living mercy as he dies for us on the cross that we might have eternal life, he clearly reveals to us and summarizes in himself the tender compassion and constant mercy of God toward his people.

One fundamental motive for practicing works of mercy has its constant roots in the Old Testament and appears consistently in the New Testament preaching. The *Book of Proverbs* teaches us: "By kindliness and loyalty, atonement is made for sin; with the fear of Yahweh goes avoidance of evil" (Pr 16:6 cf.: Si 3:30).

Giving alms, one specific work of mercy which came to stand in a general way for all works of mercy to alleviate the miseries of the less fortunate, however, can lead to an abuse. The impression could be given and a practice encouraged that by giving alms or performing other acts of mercy, one could buy forgiveness, pardon and an easy way to eternal life. Yet, implicit in this long practice encouraged in the Old and New Testaments is that every act of mercy should depend on the inner spirit that motivates it.

Another motive that aids in performing works of mercy is that such mercy gives power to our prayer and fasting before God. St. Cyprian cites Tobit 12:8-9 to show "that our prayers and our fasts lack power if they are not supported by almsgiving. Our requests cannot by themselves obtain but very little unless they are complemented by deeds and works." That is why alms during the Eucharistic Celebration on Sunday and during Lent show how sincere our prayers to God are and how effective they will be when we ask God for our needs.

The message taught in the New Testament is that by giving alms to the poor, one becomes rich with a treasure stored up in Heaven. This is the central teaching of the eschatological discourse of Jesus in Matthew 25:34ff.: "Come, you whom my Father has blessed, take for your heritage the kingdom prepared for you since the foundation of the world. For I was hungry and you gave me food. . . ."

Here we see the revolutionary view taught by Christ and held out as the more perfect motive for doing works of mercy. This motive is that we truly do to Christ whatever we do to others. If we show mercy to any human being through the corporal or spiritual works, we are assured from Christ's teaching in the New Testament and, also, by all Christians that we really do it to Christ. "I tell you solemnly, insofar as you did this to one of the least of these brothers of mine, you did it to me" (Mt 25:40).

We are made according to God's very own image and likeness (Gn 1:26), and God is mercy by his very nature as he condescends in his humility to bring us his active mercy by his caring deeds and gifts. We Christians have always felt that we demonstrate that we are really children of God (1 Jn 3:1) and have been regenerated by God's Spirit of love (Jn 3:3, 5), by our godly works of goodness and mercy, done especially to the most needy and destitute. Such mercy is the true test and validation of all other Christian virtues, since it *is* true, godly love, which embraces all other virtues and from which all other virtues flow. Yet, mercy is only such love in action, as we seek in loving compassion to help others in their miseries, as God comes to our aid in our miseries.

The Corporal Works Of Mercy

THE TRUE TEST of whether one is Christian was determined by the first century Christian communities as active mercy shown universally to any and all human persons, according to their needs and the Christian's resources and talents to respond actively to alleviate such sufferings and miseries. This was to imitate the way of life Jesus embraced. It was to obey his commands to love all others as he has loved us. "A man can have no greater love than to lay down his life for his friends" (Jn 15:13).

The first Christian communities showed mercy by first mutually pardoning each other and seeking reconciliation of one another (Col 3:13). They gave alms (Ac 9:36; 10:2, 4, 31). They were to show hospitality to those in need (1 Tm 5:10). They were to bury the dead (Ac 8:2) since the body of a Christian is a temple of the Holy Spirit (1 Cor 3:16; 6:19). It did not take long to organize works of mercy. Deacons and deaconesses were appointed to handle the distribution of alms justly, according to need, and to do all charitable actions that were needed to respond to all the necessities of one's brother or sister.

At first, there was no prescribed list of works of mercy, especially in the physical order, but a great variety of suggested works came to the fore and the daily practice of the early Christians. Gradually, writers gathered out of the Last Judgment discourse of *Matthew 25* the six corporal works of mercy and added another, that of burying the dead. In this way, Christian tradition has passed down from Christ's teaching in *Matthew 25* concrete works of mercy, without holding exclusively that only these were to be done by Christians.

The list, therefore, gives us as the corporal works of mercy: To feed the hungry, to give drink to the thirsty, to clothe the naked, to harbor the harborless, to visit the sick, to redeem captives, and to bury the dead. These were meant to be examples and incentives to embrace whatever works of mercy the moment would suggest. Christians were daily to cultivate works of mercy as essential to the spiritual life. Such Christians were not to merely wait for a chance to do good. Mercy through good works was to be pursued as a loving service rendered to Christ himself. The more one acted mercifully, the more such a Christian would wish to do. It was considered a privilege to return God's infinite mercy shown to Christians by showing mercy to all who came to them in need.

The Spiritual Works Of Mercy

ALONG with the traditional list of corporal works of mercy, we have inherited a similar list drawn from Scripture to cover works of mercy that touch individuals in their psychic and spiritual needs. These spiritual works are: to admonish the sinner, to instruct the ignorant, to counsel the doubtful, to comfort the sorrowful, to bear wrongs patiently, to forgive all injuries, and to pray for the living and the dead.

It is difficult to draw distinct lines that would separate corporal works of mercy from the spiritual ones. But we can recognize that, although in some dramatic cases the corporal works of mercy may be more compelling, still the spiritual works are more eminent than those of a corporal nature. To assist a person in his/her journey through life on its passage to eternity is more essential than many temporal acts of mercy. Yet, if a person is starving, he needs food immediately and not fraternal correction.

If we see the lists of corporal and spiritual works of mercy as containing only some suggestions of important acts of mercy, we will see the necessity on our part to go beyond any minimal works of mercy to see in the context of our daily lives what should evoke from us a generous response to the needs of our brothers and sisters, both near and far, even unknown to us by name, Christian and non-Christian.

The Privilege To Be God's Mercy To Others

WE CHRISTIANS are given the privileged responsibility, as members living "organically" in Christ, as branches inserted in a living oneness with Christ the Vine, to enflesh and extend God's mercy into all of his creation. True and intimate love of God toward us had been revealed by Jesus Christ in the Gospels as complete availability to us in our miseries, as humble love that, by grace, transforms us into mutual *I-Thou* relationships with the Trinity, this shown by the self-sacrifice of God's very self in the death of Jesus for our sakes.

We are called to build the Body of Christ throughout this world by works of mercy that manifest a similar love of availability to all in need, mutual respect of an *I-Thou* love of compassion that avoids condescending pity and is shown by our generous self-giving to others as we sacrifice ourselves in performing works of mercy on behalf of our needy brothers and sisters.

God's presence is infinite. His love is total and perfect. His mercy is above all his works. Yet, the experience of God's presence is quite dependent on Christians releasing his love and mercy in the context of our human situation. God calls others into being by the merciful love of God in us manifested in genuine, loving mercy to those whom we encounter.

Building The Body Of Christ Through Mercy

BY YOUR LOVING ACTIONS done in loving mercy to our neighbor, no matter how insignificant the works may be, we are capable of releasing God's presence within the world by building up the Body of Christ until it will reach its consummation and Christ will appear in his fullness of glory at the end of time, and recapitulate the whole created order under himself as Head.

Through our Baptism, we have been inserted into Christ, our Head. We are to find strength to bear fruit of loving mercy to others only insofar as we abide in him as branches to the vine. By our goodness and mercy shown to others in the Spirit of the risen Jesus, we are able to incarnate his merciful love and that of the Father to those who may never have had the possibility of experiencing such divine mercy.

You are not to show mercy in your human existence to others and expect then that God will begin to show mercy to you. When you show compassionate love and mercy in deeds to others, then God's merciful love will be made manifest to others and to his world. God is by nature always loving and, therefore, always merciful in his condescending energies of love for self-giving.

When we are merciful, we unleash God's infinite mercy. God's mercy becomes incarnate and appears to the world around us. Through us, others can see and know that God is an involved, compassionate, merciful, and loving God. God's love and mercy are being perfected when we love one another (1 Jn 4:12). To show love and mercy is to unveil God's love and mercy. God's greatest perfection, his very own nature as mercy, is most manifested when we show merciful love to others.

An Involving Loving Mercy

TODAY, more than ever, with the communication media allowing us to be "present" to billions of people around the world, we Christians cannot but be concerned with the rampant poverty — physical, psychic and spiritual — that covers most human beings like a suffocating black cloud. We cannot muffle our ears and block out the cries of our suffering sisters and brothers, wherever in the world they may be victims of oppression, wars or natural calamities.

Dr. Albert Schweitzer said repeatedly that as long as there was a single person in the world who was hungry, sick, lonely or living in fear, that person was his own responsibility. He truly showed us an example of a human person who released the loving mercy of God into this world through his own human involvement with the suffering people of Africa.

We know that our faith in God's love for us and our "affective" return of that love to God by words alone are dead without an "effective" involvement in manifesting unselfish love to others in need. "If one of the brothers or one of the sisters is in need of clothes and has not enough food to live on, and one of you says to them, 'I wish you well, keep yourself warm and eat plenty,' without giving them these bare necessities of life, then what good is that? Faith is like that; if good works do not go with it, it is quite dead" (Jm 2:15-17).

How we will enflesh God's mercy through our works of mercy will depend greatly on our talents and state of life, on our place and time in the Body of Christ. But openness to the world community is the sign of merciful love, a sign of one's Christian growth process in leading others to find their true identity as beautiful, worthwhile persons.

We lose our credibility as Christians, if we go to prayer before God and do not return more humble and more joyfully concerned with the anguish and sufferings of our neighbors around us. We need to allow the anguished cry for justice that rises from suffering human beings around the world first arise from the depths of our being, as we struggle with their burdens and realize that their lot is ours, that their sufferings are our sufferings. What affects others must affect us, also, and deeply so.

We really need to be pained and humbled that we cannot do anything noticeable when we see on TV part of the 450 million human beings, men, women and children, who are undernourished or facing starvation. The Synod of

Bishops meeting in Rome in 1971 issued the following statement in union with the Pope: "In the face of the present-day world situation, marked by the grave sin of injustice, we recognize our responsibility and our inability to overcome it by our own strength. . . . Such a situation urges us to listen with a humble and open heart to the word of God, as he shows us new paths toward action on behalf of justice in the world" (*The Pope Speaks*; p. 381).

What concrete action we individually will take to bring God's compassion and mercy to bear upon those situations in which we find our sisters and brothers suffering, physically, psychologically and spiritually, around the world, will vary with each person. But we cannot turn away without becoming concerned. God's mercy and love will not be revealed in our world, unless we incarnate it through our merciful works. How simply and, yet, powerfully, John expresses this in his First Epistle:

> This has taught us love:
> that he gave us his life for us;
> and we, too, ought to give up our lives for our brothers.
> If a man who was rich enough in this world's goods
> saw that one of his brothers was in need,
> but closed his heart to him,
> how could the love of God be living in him?
> My children,
> our love is not to be just words or mere talk,
> but something real and active. . . .
> His commandments are these:
> that we believe in the name of his Son, Jesus Christ,
> and that we love one another as he told us to.
> Whoever keeps his commandments
> lives in God and God lives in him.
> We know that he lives in us
> by the Spirit that he has given us (1 Jn 3:16-20-23-24).

CHAPTER EIGHT

A World In Need Of Mercy

One of my favorite authors is Nikos Kazantzakis, the Greek poet and novelist. In his *Zorba the Greek*, he gives us a powerful insight as to what is at the heart of our modern dilemma of power versus true gentleness of spirit.

> I remembered one morning when I discovered a cocoon in the bark of a tree, just as a butterful was making a hole in its case and preparing to come out. I waited a while, but it was too long appearing and I was impatient. I bent over it and breathed on it to warm it. I warmed it as quickly as I could and the miracle began to happen before my eyes, faster than life. The case opened, the butterfly started slowly crawling out and I shall never forget my horror when I saw how its wings were folded back and crumpled; the wretched

butterfly tried with its whole trembling body to unfold them. Bending over it, I tried to help it with my breath. In vain.

It needed to be hatched out patiently and the unfolding of the wings should be a gradual process in the sun. Now it was too late. My breath had forced the butterfly to appear, all crumpled, before its time. It struggled desperately and, a few seconds later, died in the palm of my hand.

That little body is, I do believe, the greatest weight I have on my conscience. For I realized today that it is a mortal sin to violate the great laws of nature. We should not hurry, we should not be impatient, but we should confidently obey the eternal rhythm.

In a way, the whole material world is like a chrysalis inside a cocoon. We, who have been made by God according to his very own image and likeness (Gn 1:26), have been given by God the command to harmonize and co-create with him this universe. We are called to be a midwife as we stand over God's material creation, that is "groaning in travail," as St. Paul describes our "not-yetness" (Rm 8:22). We impatiently breathe upon this world of such enriching gifts of God. We want the miracle of a better world to appear suddenly before our very eyes. We resort to force and even violence to get quick results.

We lack God's brooding Spirit of love that, we see on the very first page of the Bible, hovers over the chaos (Gn 1:2) with love and condescending mercy. We need to get in touch with "the eternal rhythm" of God's silent pulse of his love permeating actively all of his creation. He brings forth all creatures in silence and non-violence. His love is "always patient and kind . . . it is always ready to excuse, to trust, to hope, and to endure whatever comes" (1 Cor 13:4-7).

A World With Little Mercy

Ours is a world drunk with power. We fear so very much any sign of mercy because we believe it a sign of weakness. We have placed ourselves, instead of God, at the center of the universe. We have accepted, unquestioningly, as our teacher, Nietzsche, who convinces us that the will to power is the key to fulfillment. According to his principle anything that springs from weakness is bad.

The poet, Tagore, a decade before World War II, voiced the problem which is still very much at the heart of our contemporary world:

> Civilization... has lost its balance and is moving by hopping from war to war. Its motive forces are the forces of destruction and its ceremonials are carried through by an apalling number of human sacrifices. This... civilization is crashing along a series of catastrophes at a tremendous speed....

In our new age of technology and instant communication with the entire universe by satellites, we are tensioned between a feeling of pessimism, even fear, and an optimism that excites us with fanciful dreams of a world of infinite richness. In a way, our universe is shrinking in the sense of all parts of it becoming more and more "present" to our fellow human beings. Yet, in a way, we stand in a frightened isolation "against" that unknown world, exploding before us into mysteries that we cannot handle with our limited human knowledge.

A Created Frankenstein

ALONG with the riches produced by modern technology, we have also created our own Frankenstein. We have let loose in our world a demonic force that is blanketing the universe with a destructive power that propels us toward a universal cataclysm at an alarming rate each day. Our earth's deposits of natural resources are rapidly being consumed, leaving slag heaps in oceans of garbage. Fumes from man's machines rise up to cloud the atmoshpere with a gaseous curtain that is affecting the ozone layer and could eventually throttle any green life on planet earth.

And so we stand frightened before such apocalyptic visions of a doomed planet earth. What happened to God's loving children, made a little less than a god (Ps 8:5), who once danced joyously to soft music, thrilled to climb snowcapped mountains, loved to break bread with friends and enjoy a glass of wine together?

There is a universal *angst* or sense of anxiety that fills the hearts of us modern human beings with a feeling of meaninglessness to our lives. Our immersion in a pragmatic materialism has suffocated our communion with God's gentle Spirit of love and mercy. Cut off from an experienced, interpersonal relationship in faith, hope and love, we, with God and with each other, are adrift on a dark, stormy ocean that threatens our very own sanity.

Need For Mercy

THE Vatican Council II Pastoral Constitution on the *Church in the Modern World* summarized for us the tension we live under, between seeming-human power and our own finite weaknesses and even sinfulness: "In the light of the foregoing factors, there appears the dichotomy of a world that is at once powerful and weak, capable of doing what is noble and what is base, disposed to freedom and slavery, progress and decline, brotherhood and hatred. Man is growing conscious that the forces he has unleashed are in his own hands and that it is up to him to control them or be enslaved by them" (#9).

Pope John Paul II on November 30, 1980, published his encyclical *Rich in Mercy (Dives in Misericordia)*, in which he quite accurately describes our modern world as one that has excluded the very notion of mercy for rugged individualism, based on "my" rights with little sense of the common good:

> The present-day mentality, more perhaps than that of people in the past, seems opposed to a God of mercy, and in fact, tends to exclude from life and to remove from the human heart the very idea of mercy. The word and the concept of "mercy" seem to cause uneasiness in man, who, thanks to the enormous development of science and technology, never before known in history, has become the master of the earth and has subdued and dominated it. This dominion over the earth, sometimes understood in a one-sided and superficial way, seems to leave no room for mercy (#2).

Jesus Christ: God's Mercy Incarnate

THE REASON why people do not talk about mercy is that they do not think of mercy nor act mercifully. Our great disease is that we have placed ourselves instead of God at the center of our lives. We are busy in our heads creating worlds that will bring to us more money, more power, more pleasure. God created man and woman in a loving relationship with himself and with each other, to live in harmony with the entire material universe through creative work. We were endowed with the free will to live in loving union or to disobey God. Yet, we chose to be our own masters. Scripture describes the result of sin as a violation of God's established order. We human beings flee as exiles from God. But in so doing, we also run away from our true selves that can only be fulfilled in loving union in a community with others.

Because we have ignored our individual sinfulness and that of our oneness with every human being living in such sin of "bias toward self," we have, therefore, lost the concept and the experience of God's mercy toward us. We blithely ignore the "spiritual army of evil" (Ep 6:12) that enforces darkness upon all of us in all generations. The accumulated brokenness shows itself in our own existential situation in which we presently live.

We are being sucked down into its dark pits continuously in our families, in our culture, in our economic and political arenas, and even in our churches. Like a poisonous gas that infiltrates every molecule of air, we "breathe in" sin and selfishness in every waking moment. The law of the jungle is within our very bones and all around us exerting its tyrannical power over us. The same law, enforced by the "lord of the flies," is within us, beating us slaves into a quivering submission.

We will never truly understand mercy until we understand that God is gracious and merciful toward us individually and that his mercy is above all his works. And we will never come to know what God's mercy means to us and be transformed by that mercy to live mercifully toward all others whom we encounter, unless we believe in Jesus Christ as the God-Man, who images the merciful Father. St. Paul beautifully summarizes for us God's plan to restore us from a world of sin and violence to God's world of harmony in loving service toward each other by revealing to us the richness of God's mercy in Jesus Christ.

> But God, who is rich in mercy, was moved by the intense love with which he loved us, and when we were dead by reason of our transgressions, he made us live with the life of Christ. By grace you have been saved. Together with Christ Jesus and in him, he raised us up and enthroned us in the heavenly realm, that in Christ Jesus he might show throughout the ages to come the overflowing riches of his grace springing from his goodness to us. Yes, it is by grace that you have been saved through faith; it is the gift of God; it is not the result of anything you did, so that no one has any grounds for boasting. We are his handiwork, created in Christ Jesus in view of good deeds which God prepared beforehand for us to practice (Ep 2:4-10).

Jesus, God's Love Enfleshed

THE GREAT SIN in all our lives is disbelief that God truly does love us and shows infinite, pefect mercy by condescending to come among us and to die out of merciful love for each of us. We will continue to live by violence toward others and even God and retreat into the isolation of our hellish world where we live by loneliness, unless we can allow ourselves in faith, hope and love to be transformed by Jesus Christ as God's loving mercy, enfleshed and living intimately within us.

The Good News is that in Jesus Christ, God and Man, God's mercy has become visible to us. The Father in the Old Testament is seen as truly "rich in mercy" (Ep 2:4). The prophets reveal to us a God, who is concerned with every detail of our earthly existence. His mercy is above all his works (Ps 145:9). "As a father has compassion on his children, so has the Lord compassion on them that fear him" (Ps 103:13). "But he is merciful, and will forgive their sins" (Ps 78:38).

But, it is only when God, who so loved us, gave us his only begotten Son, that we can have life in him (Jn 3:16) and that we are able to know that God the Father is love and mercy toward us. Jesus is not merely merciful by his merciful acts toward us, but in a way, he images the nature of the unseen God (Col 1:15). In Jesus, we know that God's love, goodness, holiness, righteousness and mercy are not merely extrinsic perfections of God, but that these are descriptions of God's constant and unchanging nature, as we have pointed out in detail in the early chapters of this book. God does not possess the perfection of love or mercy by beginning to act in such a manner toward us. God *is* love. He does not begin to love us and show mercy to us in our brokenness, especially when we ask for his forgiving mercy, and then cease to act in such a manner.

God loves us as Jesus does. God's mercy is revealed in the manner that Jesus shows mercy to us in his earthly life. When the Word became flesh and pitched his tent among us

(Jn 1:14), God had definitively spoken his Word in the person of Jesus Christ. ". . . But in our own time, the last days, he has spoken to us through his Son, the Son that he has appointed to inherit everything and through whom he made everything there is. He is the radiant light of God's glory and the perfect copy of his nature, sustaining the universe by his powerful command. . . ." (Heb 1:2-3).

The Silent Word Of God

JESUS CAME among us in human form to communicate to us in human language God's plan for us. He told us about the Heavenly Father. He described to us how infinite is the Father's love and care for each of us. He told us that we, too, were destined to share in his very own life and to be one in him forever with the Father. He would pour out his Spirit, who would take away our sins and regenerate us with a rebirth from above (Jn 3:3, 5), so that we could really become children of the Heavenly Father (1 Jn 3:1).

But his greatest work was not to speak words, but to become the silent Word of God, as he poured out his life for love of us on the cross. Contemplating Jesus poured out on the cross, we can see how great is the Father's loving mercy toward us. By dying and passing over into a new creation, Jesus was empowered by his Father to pour out his Spirit, who would bear united witness to our spirit that we are truly children of God, co-heirs with Christ forever (Rm 8:15; Gal 4:6).

St. Bernard beautifully describes how Jesus is the Father's mercy for us and in him we are made righteous:

Through these sacred wounds we can see the secret of his heart, the great mystery of love, the sincerity of his *mercy* with which he visited us from on high. Where have your mercy, your compassion shone out more luminously than in your wounds, sweet, gentle Lord of mercy? More mercy than this no one has than that he lay down his life for those who are doomed to death (Sermon 61:3-5).

Dark Forces Warring Against Mercy

THE WAY of the humble Jesus in showing us mercy, in order that we might be healed of our pride and sinfulness and show mercy to others, is clearly symbolized in his washing of the feet of the disciples before he went to his suffering and death. He acts out for his disciples and for all of us, his followers, the symbol of how God, the Master, stoops down in compassionate mercy to wash away our sins, relieves us from our body, soul and spiritual sufferings and infirmities and, in forgiving love, to restore us to our human dignity as happy and whole children of God. We are able, through his Holy Spirit, once Jesus died and rose from the dead, to understand the meaning of Jesus' death that would bring us a total cleansing from all sin which comes from self-centeredness, driven by power, and not mercy, to dominate God and neighbor. St. John writes in his epistle:

> But if we shape our conduct in the atmosphere of his light as he himself is in light, we have union with one another, and the blood of Jesus, his Son, cleanses us from every stain of sin (1 Jn 1:7).

We have a need, before we can be converted to show mercy to others, to be converted away from the world's standard of values. Paul calls these values, "illusory desires" (Ep 4:23). They must be fought against and be put to death by "a going against" (*agere contra*, as St. Ignatius in his *Spiritual Exercises* describes such forces) the values that build up our false self. This is the therapy necessary before we can positively put on the mind of Jesus Christ, "renewed by a spiritual revolution" (Ep 4:24) by first putting aside our old self (Ep 4:23).

We are in great need to discern the stratagems of the inimical forces within ourselves and around us in our social and religious institutions that keep us in bondage to sin and, therefore, force us to be unmerciful toward others in our self-absorption. Before we can habitually be merciful toward others, we must become aware of the tempting elements within us and around us in society and in our western culture as a whole that crush out or at least effectively defeat our best desires to be merciful as God is.

St. Ignatius, both from his long meditations in Scripture and his personal reflections on his own sins and temptations, powerfully, with great insight and simplicity, presents to us, in his *Spiritual Exercises*, the thinking of the "world." In his well-known meditation on the *Two Standards*, or two strategies that are presented to us for our choice to follow one or the other, Ignatius shows the various intermingling of spirits, both good and evil, impacting us at all times. Good and evil forces are both at work in us, like light and darkness, truth and deception, life and death. The two leaders who seek our undivided allegiance, are Christ and the "enemy."

The strategy of the "enemy" is:

> First . . . to tempt people to covet riches, as he (the enemy) is ordinarily accustomed to do, that they may the more easily attain the empty honors of the world, and then come to swollen pride. The first step, then, will be riches, the second honor, the third, pride. And from these three steps, he leads to all the other vices (*Sp. Ex.* 142).

Christ's strategy that will lead us to be merciful love in service toward all others is to:

> Seek to help all, by attracting them, first to the highest spiritual poverty and, if his divine Majesty should so be served and he should wish to choose them for it, even to actual poverty. Secondly, they should lead them to a desire for insults and contempt, for from these two things follows humility. Hence, there will be three steps: the first, poverty, as opposed to riches; the second, insults and contempt, as opposed to worldly honor; the third, humility, as opposed to pride. And from these three steps, let them lead them to all the other virtues (*Sp. Ex* 146).

The Spirit of Jesus develops in us a style of life such as Jesus lived, and image of the triune God's nature as merciful love to his human creatures. As Jesus was poor, merciful and compassionate toward all the poor, oppressed, dehumanized persons who came to him, so we are invited to have a part with him. But to be loving mercy to all, we will have to deny our false selves and be ready to embrace the "cross," the symbol of all sufferings that accompany our attempts to live with mercy toward all others.

This is the condition Jesus lays down, if we are to have a part with him in eternal life in God's kingdom: "If anyone wants to be a follower of mine, let him renounce himself and take up his cross and follow me. For anyone who wants to save his life will lose it; but anyone, who loses his life for my sake and for the sake of the gospel, will save it" (Mk 8:34; Mt 10:38; Lk 9:23).

Loving Mercy Beyond Justice

THIS MEANS that we are asked by Jesus to go beyond mere justice to embrace a life of loving service toward others. This makes us vulnerable to be rejected in our mercy and love shown toward others. Jesus promises that we will be asked to be ready to receive rejection, humiliations, persecutions on his behalf. Our reaction to this? We are to rejoice and dance with God, for by such we enter into the Kingdom of God. We come into God's real world through humility (Lk 6:23).

The enemy offers to us an opposing way that the majority of us find at the basis of our temptations to move away from being merciful to others, toward independence and merciless, violent actions.

Riches are material goods, symbolized in the West as money or personal wealth. Our very mobile western world offers us individualistic power in our insecurity before a threatening world of anonymity. Such power is attained in the possession of material things. In our modern capitalistic society, the most immediate and socially accepted path to self-centered security, lies in storing up money or things that seemingly assure us of our independence. "More ain't enough!" is the cry in our consumeristic world which then wars against sharing such riches with others who are hungry, homeless and inhumanly oppressed and degraded because they lack such accepted signs of power and security.

Worldly Success

SUCH RICHES bring honors and a sense of importance within human society. It is a short step from such honors to deeply entrenched pride. Such pride manifests the utter lack of mercy shown toward the needy by corporal and spiritual works of compassionate service. Pride assumes the concrete attitudes of arrogance, selfish ambition in the henpecking competition in ascending the ladder of "success," and a superiority complex toward all others.

The model of success appears to be the "famous" persons: movie and sports stars, politicians and sex symbols, people who project an image of success through money, honors and "the credit of a great name." While the "poor people" are considered as the shiftless outcasts of society, the mentally and physically handicapped, the aliens, the homeless, the bag ladies; in a word, every person whom we find living in misery and human indignity and from whom we turn away and refuse to show mercy.

The Way Of Christ

JESUS IS the *Way*, the *Truth* and the *Life* (Jn 14:6). His way, as we have seen is God's way of relating to his children. His way is the way of non-condemnation, of active mercy shown to all of us in all our miseries and needs. In order to follow Jesus and extend his mercy into the time and place of our historical world, we need, first, a radical conversion and healing of our values in order to accept the values Jesus lived by and which he still teaches his followers to embrace.

He calls us to become poor in spirit and to swing free of all inordinate attachments to things. This does not mean to live in want or destitution. It does mean that we are detached from what we do not really need so we can freely share with all who are in greater need than we ourselves. We enter into a state of true freedom and harmonious integration, as we see God's *Logos* in each created gift given to us, to be guided by that Word in whom all things are created (Jn 1:3). We become responsible stewards and no longer "owners" of private property. We no longer say and think: This is *mine.* I give it to you," but, "This is *ours; you* need it more than I. Take what is *yours!"*

The essential characteristic of the way of Jesus and of God, that should become ours in showing mercy in all our dealing, revolves first around our identity as a unique person, loved in a special manner by the triune community of love. I will never be able to show love and mercy to other beings unless I, by the power of God's Holy Spirit, continuously experience, in deepening faith, hope and love, God's merciful love toward me.

In such personalized experiences of God as mercy in my brokenness, sinfulness and moments of lapses into selfishness, I move freely away from a false identity attained from power through possessing riches, honors and pride and become grounded in my unique worth, not by anything I do, or possess, but sheerly because God is so rich in mercy (Ep 2:4) and truly loves, because for me Jesus has died! Who can ever separate me from this abiding love of the indwelling Father, Son and Spirit (Rm 8:38-39)? I live at the core of my being where God is my Rock and Salvation. I am free in that love to possess my life as a beautiful gift which I can give in love and merciful service to all who come into my life.

I Am Thou, Thou Art I

THIS CHANGES my attitude toward those "others." We are no longer *I* and *them*. All become my brothers and sisters, uniquely beautiful because of God's unique way of loving them in his creative Word. No longer do I feel I am doing good deeds or favors to someone in need. *Mutuality* is the Holy Spirit's illumination that I truly am one with the other and both of us are one in Christ. We with Christ form an organism, the Church. He is the Head, we, the members.

As we individually experience God's healing love through the mercy shown us in Jesus Christ, we become healthy members of his Body. We are aware of our own unique beauty and the gifts we possess by God's goodness and by Jesus' Spirit, who builds the Body of Christ into a unity of love (Ep 4:4). To that degree of our special and healthy place in Christ's Body, we learn to respect the equality of all human persons, called by God in Christ Jesus to come into their unique beauty.

We especially come to the help of the weak members, to help them live according to the fullness of their potential for wholeness in the same Body of Christ. St. Paul writes: "... that there may not be disagreements inside the body, but that each part may be equally concerned for all the others. If one part is hurt, all parts are hurt with it. If one part is given special honor, all parts enjoy it" (1 Cor 12:25-26).

Our Christian faith-vision stresses the equality of all human beings "to liberty and the pursuit of happiness," plus the ultimate goal of building the Body of Christ, especially by doing to the least, we do also literally to Christ (Mt 25:31-46). We move away from the values of the "world" to live as Jesus lived. Our mercy and loving service extend ourselves outward in all our social relations to build a community of love by rejecting an exclusive, individualistic self-centeredness. Competition is replaced by cooperation and humble service.

Giving, We Receive

SINCE OUR TRUST is in God, our strength, we can live in a state of being a pilgrim, detached from the urge to find our identity in the exclusive possession of things, to move freely under the Spirit to be a brother or sister to all others whom we meet. Such detachment permits us to experience the fulfillment of Jesus' promise: "Anyone who loves his life loses it; anyone who hates his life in this world will keep it for the eternal life" (Jn 12:25).

Filled with loving mercy, as Jesus was toward the outcasts of society, we soon learn that our giving to the poor, the miserable ones of society, is never uni-directional. The outcasts of society, in a way, offer us their loving mercy. As God loves the "lowly" and abides among the poor and the helpless, so he uses them to break down our illusions, the worlds we have created to maintain a world of *us* and *them*, of those who *have* and those who *have not*. When we lose our life in this "world," we find our true selves and have already eternal life. This cannot be done unless we associate with the lot of the poor and despised.

This losing of our life in this world (Jn 12:25) puts to

death any pride as it inclines us toward the cross of humiliations and insults, persecutions and sufferings, that come with our sharing, as Jesus did, the lot of the oppressed. In the early Church (and even now in some totalitarian countries), Christians were and are called at any moment to lay down their lives in physical martyrdom for their belief that Jesus Christ is truly God!

Identifying With The Oppressed

TODAY, all Christians in the Body of Christ are called to a different, but no less demanding, form of martyrdom as they are called to identify themselves with the oppressed of the world. There is no other way for us to lose our illusory power over things than to seek actually to be so one with the oppressed that we are ready to bear their humiliations.

We do not seek such "crosses" in themselves. The paradox is that we seek to show true mercy toward those in greatest misery and we will always have to endure a part of their persecutions, rejection, injuries from the more "powerful" and merciless ones.

Jesus promised that we would be persecuted, if we chose to live as he did.

> Blessed are you when the world hates you,
> and bars you from its society, and reviles you,
> and brands you as criminals — and that for
>   the sake of the Son of Man.
> Rejoice at such moments; yes, leap for joy!
> Mark my words: there is a rich reward
> for you in heaven (Lk 6:22-23).

No one can provide us with a static blueprint, as Jesus himself never did, of what we concretely have to do in order to show mercy to the outcasts. Associating with the poor and despised does not mean we give up our talents, our gifts, including money and other objective riches. What true mercy means is that in the working to build a loving community, the Body of Christ, others and the community have precedence over our own self-centered interests. God is at the center of our lives and gives us the strength to "enflesh" his merciful love through service to all others who come into our lives.

A Modern Need For Mercy

OUR PRESENT WORLD desperately needs to be guided by Christ's values of loving God with our whole heart and loving our neighbor as ourselves. We individually and as nations need to relinquish the power of aggrandizement through violence and begin to trust in the basic goodness, dignity and beauty of each human person. We need to turn swords into plows to cultivate the riches of this world through true mercy shown to each person, regardless of race, color, creed, sex, education, financial worth, or status.

Then, we will reach that state where even mercy will be transformed into love and only three things will remain: "There are three things that last: faith, hope and love; and the greatest of these is love" (1 Cor 13:13).

Prayer To Jesus For Mercy

Dearest Jesus, Lover of mankind: I come before you as you hang on the cross. You are the incarnate image of the Father's forgiving mercy toward his children, who have turned away from his outpouring love. For love of me, you did not grasp at your omnipotent divinity, but you emptied yourself as a servant, even unto the last drop of water and blood (Ph 2:8; Jn 19:25). "Without beauty, without majesty, no looks to attract our eyes; a thing despised and rejected by men" (Is 53:2-3).

Like the publican of the Gospel, I am overcome with sorrow and shame, as I see the sins and brokenness of my life rise up before me. I can only bow my head and cry with childlike trust for your forgiving mercy: "God, be merciful to me, a sinner!" (Lk 18:14). I have been locked in the darkness of my inner blindness, but, like Bartimaeus, I make bold to cry unto you: "Jesus, Son of David, have pity on me!" (Lk 18:39).

With the penitent King David, I too cry out:

> Have mercy on me, O God, in your goodness,
> in your great tenderness wipe away my faults;
> wash me clean of my guilt,
> purify me from my sin.
>
> For I am well aware of my faults,
> I have my sin constantly in mind,
> having sinned against none other than you,
> having done what you regard as wrong.
>
> You are just when you pass sentence on me,
> blameless when you give judgment.
> You know I was born guilty,
> a sinner from the moment of conception.
>
> Yet, since you love sincerity of heart,
> teach me the secrets of wisdom.
> Purify me with hyssop until I am clean;
> wash me until I am whiter than snow.
>
> Instill some joy and gladness into me,
> let the bones you have crushed rejoice again.
> Hide your face from my sins,
> wipe out all my guilt.
>
> God, create a clean heart in me,
> put into me a new and constant spirit,
> do not banish me from your presence,
> do not deprive me of your holy spirit (Ps 51:1-11).

As I look into your blood-stained eyes, O Lord, Jesus Christ, Son of God, I confess with sinful David: "I have sinned against Yahweh" (2 S 12:13). May you speak from your cross the words of the prophet, Nathan, addressed to the penitent David: "Yahweh, for his part, forgives your sins; you are not to die" (2 S 12:14).

Prayer To Jesus For Mercy

I crouch in the depths of my inner darkness, while the specter of despair haunts me. Fears and tremors, sorrows, cares and guilt attack me endlessly. I strike now here, now there at enemies who, as invisible forces, beat me into hopeless prison-like confinement.

I cry in the dark night as a lost child, because I feel I am alone in my darkness and fear. Speak to me, my loving Savior, your words, which you uttered to your Heavenly Father, as you hung in agony on the cross: "Father, forgive them; they do not know what they are doing" (Lk 23:34).

O, most sweet Jesus, it is only to you I can come with confidence, not in my past actions, but solely because I believe you are the mercy of the Father, made flesh, and that I can draw near to you and be touched by you and hear the words you addressed to the adulterous woman: "Neither do I condemn you" (Jn 8:11).

Dearest Jesus, Image of the Father, I am in urgent need of your forgiving mercy for all the sins of my past life. I bring to you, Divine Physician, sent by the Father, that I might be healed, all the brokenness of my life. Set me free from sin and death, in order that I might come home to your Father, and my Father, and enjoy more abundant life, eternal life, even now! I cast all my evils, guilt and fears, despair of not ever receiving your pardon, into the abyss of your divine mercy and grace.

Grant me to enter into your pierced heart and, by your outpoured blood, may I be cleansed of all my sins and of death in order to rise into a new oneness with you, a new creation!

O Jesus, so worthy of all my love, my only source of strength and comfort, of healing and forgiving love, I stand at the foot of your cross in the company of your Mother, Mary, the penitent, Mary Magdalene, and your beloved disciple. I pray that your Mother, Mary, will intercede for me and teach me how to allow you in your mercy to speak your word in my life and I will do it according to your will. May she show me that your name is holy and your mercy reaches from age to age for those who fear you (Lk 1:49-50).

May I have the repentance of Mary Magdalene from whom you drove out seven evil spirits and who washed your feet with her tears of sorrow and anointed them with precious ointment.

May John, the beloved disciple, teach me how to rest on your breast and experience the powerful love of your pierced heart, transforming me also into your beloved disciple.

I look about me and see the darkening clouds of despair that cover the passersby of this world who do not believe that your mercy is above all your works. Men and women, and even children, need your forgiving and healing mercy so much, for they see so little of mercy in our times.

Fill my heart with deep compassion and loving mercy for so many people who are slaves of their fears and do not know how beautiful they could be if they would only accept your infinite mercy. Lord, Jesus Christ, Son of God, have mercy on me and on them! Have mercy on all of us and forgive us for our collective sinfulness, living by violence in our thoughts and deeds. Forgive our nation and our leaders for their lack of mercy toward the oppressed, the outcasts of society among the homeless, the hungry, the mentally sick, the lonely elderly, and those in prison. Forgive them for not being good stewards over the abundant riches you give to our country by sharing your gifts with Third World countries, especially with the 480 million starving because they lack proper nutrition, for the millions who have lost all hope that they can be restored to the proper dignity fitting all children of your loving Father. For all these, you have died!

Be mercy to us all and heal us that, by your outpoured love, we may be transformed to extend your mercy to a broken world. May we give your healing love to all whom we meet. Accept us to be your hands and feet to go where you, in your omnipotence, can no longer go among the broken ones of this world, your world.

We are broken, but your mercy is able to heal us so we can step out in faith to be broken healers by your infinite mercy to a broken world that knows not that you are gracious and merciful, and that your mercy endures forever! Amen! Amen!

An Interesting Thought

The publication you have just finished reading is part of the apostolic efforts of the Society of St. Paul of the American Province. The Society of St. Paul is an international religious community located in 23 countries, whose particular call and ministry is to bring the message of Christ to all people through the communications media.

Following in the footsteps of their patron, St. Paul the Apostle, priests and brothers blend a life of prayer and technology as writers, editors, marketing directors, graphic designers, bookstore managers, pressmen, sound engineers, etc. in the various fields of the mass media, to announce the message of Jesus.

If you know a young man who might be interested in a religious vocation as a brother or priest and who shows talent and skill in the communications arts, ask him to consider our life and ministry. For more information at no cost or obligation write:

>   Vocation Office
>   2187 Victory Blvd.
>   Staten Island, NY 10314-6603
>   Telephone: (718) 698-3698